The Working Parent Dilemma

The Working Parent Dilemma

How to Balance the Responsibilities of Children and Careers

Earl A. Grollman
Gerri L. Sweder

Beacon Press • Boston

Beacon Press
25 Beacon Street
Boston, Massachusetts 02108-2892
www.beacon.org

Beacon Press books
are published under the auspices of
the Unitarian Universalist Association of Congregations.

First digital-print edition 2001

Library of Congress Cataloging-in-Publication Data
Grollman, Earl A.
The working parent dilemma.
ISBN 0-8070-2703-0
1. Children of working parents—United States. 2. Work and family—United States. 3.
Latchkey children—United States. I. Sweder, Gerri L. II. Title.
HQ777.6.G76   1986
306.8′   85-47941

With Love

To Netta
and my grandchildren,
Jennifer, Eric, and Aaron
E.A.G.

To Ken
and my children,
Justin and Rebecca
G.L.S.

Contents

Acknowledgments

We are deeply grateful to:
the thousand children who shared their feelings, thoughts, and ideas. Their words and their warmth remain with us.

Henry David Abraham, M.D., Department of Psychiatry, Harvard Medical School, for his probing questions and insights, which enabled us to more clearly define our goals.

Ruth MacDonald, formerly co-director, Center for Family Strengths of the Educational Development Center of Massachusetts and Nebraska, for her invaluable assistance in helping us to distribute our questionnaires to children across the country.

Alvin Fortune, principal, Brookline, Massachusetts, and Francis Manzelli, principal, Watertown, Massachusetts, and the many other principals and teachers who opened up their schools and whose opinions and experiences broadened and deepened our own understanding of the needs of children of two working parents.

Sharon Grollman and Jane Cullen for their many hours of reading and editing the manuscript, for their discerning suggestions, organizational ability, skill with language, and subtle understanding of what we wished to convey.

Wendy Strothman, director, Beacon Press, for her creative advice and recommendations, which guided us in the completion of our book and for giving structure to our many ideas.

Andrew Maddocks, Ph.D., and Mark Palmerino, doctoral student in social psychology, Harvard University, for helping us design and evaluate the children's surveys, which provided us with the research material for more thoroughly assessing children's attitudes.

Dedicated friends, who endured exhaustive conversation about the book while being supportive and encouraging.

Family members, including parents and parents-in-law, for their devotion and love.

Kenneth Sweder, for his reassuring words, his loving patience, his thoughtfulness, and his belief in this book. He is a working father who is truly committed and involved in his children's daily lives.

Justin and Rebecca Sweder, who provided needed hugs and kisses along with wonderful ideas and their own very definite thoughts on living with two working parents.

Netta Grollman, for her continuing understanding, gentleness, and caring as wife and mother.

David, Sharon, and Jonathan Grollman, who have been teachers to better parenting.

And all others who have helped along the way.

Introduction

The definition of childhood and of the "average" American family is changing throughout the country. In the past, the "average" American family was thought to comprise two children under age eighteen, an employed father, and a housewife mother. Today, that description fits only 5 percent of American families. The typical elementary school child today lives with two employed parents; the same is true for over half of all preschool children. Twenty years ago there were about nineteen million two-job families; ten years ago there were almost twenty-two and a half million; and today there are over twenty-six million and the numbers continue to rise.

We were surprised to find relatively little research on the child's point of view. Recently, several books and magazine articles have focused on how parents can combine work and family life. Much of the advice has concerned meeting the needs of the parents. (The expression *working parents* is awkward. Parents who stay home with children are obviously working, but the scope of our book is limited to the child whose parents are employed, usually outside the home. The term *working parents* is used in this sense.) Parents who want to better ensure an emotionally healthy childhood need to hear about the views of these youngsters before they can more successfully arrange their own adult lives and responsibilities. This book is therefore addressed to the working parents struggling to raise a child in this new environment. This book is written, in large part, from the child's point of view.

For both parent and child, family life has changed dramatically. All of these parents face *The Working Parent Dilemma* — trying to successfully balance work and family life. One of the most disturbing trends has been the increase in youngsters who spend time at home without adult supervision. A recent *Newsweek* article reported "that perhaps 5 million American children under the age of 10 have no one to look after them when they come home in the afternoon. By some estimates, 500,000 preschoolers under the age of six are in a similar predicament." One ten-year-old summed up the dilemma of many youngsters when he said to us, "My parents say I'm old enough to be by myself. But I'm scared being home alone. I'm afraid something is going to happen to me." This child's lingering worry is echoed every day in millions of homes.

How does it feel to grow up with working parents? How do children of different ages meet and respond to these new demands? To help mothers and fathers answer these questions, we decided to consult the experts — the children themselves. As working parents involved with children in counseling and education, we were especially interested in youngsters' views about how their parents' working affected them. We therefore surveyed approximately one thousand students. All the mothers of the children we surveyed were in the work force. Some had been employed since their children were babies; others went to work when their youngsters were enrolled in preschool programs; still others joined the labor market after the youngest child entered elementary school, and some when their youngsters were older. The collective insights of the children from living with two working parents are incorporated in this book to help parents better understand how their employment affects their children's daily lives.

Students were surveyed in two groups. First, we interviewed almost four hundred students in both small and large groups. These youngsters were enrolled in elementary schools and in junior and senior high schools and were drawn from various socioeconomic and ethnic backgrounds. Some of our discussions with the children in this group concerned:

- the need for nurture and togetherness when parents returned from work
- suggestions for improving child care arrangements before and after school
- how it feels to be at home alone when parents are at work
- parents' involvement in children's lives both in and out of school
- changing views of the roles of women and men

These students were eager to share their ideas and suggestions with us. Over and over again youngsters told us of their relief at finally being able to express their innermost feelings. Some said they never before had an opportunity to voice these thoughts and concerns. Many asked if we would come back and tell them what other children had to say. One twelve-year-old declared, "I liked hearing what other kids do after school when their parents are at work."

To ensure the accuracy of the children's words, and to ease the flow of their thoughts, all conversations were tape-recorded. We have used their language in this book in both direct quotations and paraphrases. Because we promised anonymity to the youngsters, we changed their names.

To supplement the findings from our oral interviews, we devised a written Attitude Survey again specifically for children living with two employed parents. This second group comprised 641 youngsters from twenty school systems in eleven states including California, Colorado, Florida, Maryland, Massachusetts, Minnesota, Nebraska, New Jersey, New York, Texas, and Virginia. Fifty-six percent of the respondents were female; forty-four percent, male. The participating students represented all income levels and attended public and private schools in grades four, six, eight, ten, and twelve. Parents' jobs included unskilled workers, blue collar workers, clerk typists and secretaries, technical workers, managers, executives, and professionals. The written survey was anonymous, and took approximately forty minutes to complete.

Some of the questions in the written survey were designed to elicit factual information about the youngsters: "I usually go for help with my schoolwork to..." or "I have my mother's at-work phone number," or "I have my father's at-work phone number." Other questions were designed to learn about the youngsters' feelings by asking them to agree or disagree with certain statements: "I think it's good to have both parents work" or "I feel lonely being by myself after school."

The students also completed a standardized questionnaire known as the Self-Esteem Inventories, which were designed by Stanley Coopersmith to measure children's level of self-esteem in four categories: general, home, academic, and social. In addition, the students were asked to respond to a series of sixteen statements, including the Hollander Parent Contact Scale, that scored the frequency in which mothers and fathers demonstrated physical and verbal affection for their children. Finally, this group completed an open-ended imagination exercise that involved writing a conclusion to the following unfinished story:

*P.L. is a young person about my age who
lives with a family where P.L.'s mother and
father both work Monday through Friday. P.L.
is a very thoughtful young person, and after
school P.L. goes home, knowing that mother
and father won't be there until later. P.L.
starts to think...*

Giving youngsters the opportunity to share their thoughts and feelings through writing a story was a valuable experience for them and for us. Children were able to express deeply held emotions that are often not revealed on multiple-choice surveys. We were so impressed with the sensitivity and awareness in some of the stories that we have included a sample of them in an appendix. Even though the youngsters lived in different sections of the country, they echoed in surprising detail and precision the feelings of their peers hundreds or thousands of miles away.

Talking with these youngsters has been an exciting learning experience for us. They enabled us to more fully understand and meet the needs of our own children. It is our wish that our research will help parents and all those concerned with children and families to listen more sensitively and respond more effectively.

We hope mothers and fathers will find in the following pages a deeper insight into resolving *The Working Parent Dilemma* and develop a more satisfactory way of balancing work and family life. There are problems. But there are also many opportunities for creative solutions. Parents can be employed and meet the emotional, physical, and intellectual needs of their children. This requires an intense commitment by both parents to maintaining a loving, open relationship with their youngsters while creating an atmosphere in which the needs of all family members are respected.

Chapter 1

Growing Up with Working Parents— The Pros and Cons

*M*ost *children growing up* today accept as a norm the home in which both parents work. But they also expect their needs and concerns to be met by parents who know how to balance their family and work lives wisely. As we listened to children voice their feelings about living with working parents, we were impressed by their ability to recognize both advantages and disadvantages in their circumstances and to suggest ways to avoid the extremes that could harm the family. Let us look at the three main advantages in the two-job family identified by the youngsters and then at the disadvantages and specific suggestions on how to recognize and cope with them.

Having More Money

I think two parents have to work these days. My mother went back to work about five years ago when my oldest sister was in the sixth grade. My parents wanted to start saving for college for my sister and the rest

*of us. My mom says sometimes she feels like
all the money she makes is just paying for
college.*

Jonathan, age 12

Children of all ages list "making money" as the number
one reason why their parents work. Indeed, most mothers
and fathers work because of economic necessity and to assure financial stability for their children and themselves.
Maintaining a family is expensive. As Professor James
Garbarino of Pennsylvania State University states, "An
analysis by Olson (1983) concludes that the average middle-
class two-parent family setting out to raise a child in 1980
can expect to spend about $140,000 (in 1982 dollars) to raise
a child to age 22 — about 22% of its income. The estimate
for a low income family (in the twentieth percentile of the
income distribution) is about $70,000." Youngsters under-
stand that money is required to pay for food, clothing,
housing, medical bills, school supplies, and college education. "My mom and dad saved for a long time so we could
buy a nice house," an eleven-year-old remarked.

Depending on age or maturity, your child may view the
higher income in a two-job family as an opportunity to
purchase items long wished for but previously too expensive. Like adults, children want material comforts.

Although some children first notice the opportunity to
buy more personal goods such as clothes or tapes, other
children are excited about using an increase in income to
enjoy more activities as a family. Ten-year-old Andrea said,
"We eat out more often. I really like that. Everyone seems
happier, especially my mom. She doesn't have to cook or
do the dishes, so she's more relaxed." Almost two thirds
of the elementary school children we interviewed stated
that their families are able to take longer, more frequent,
or more unusual trips since their mothers returned to work

outside the home. They think of vacations as rewards parents give themselves and their children for hard work. Thirteen-year-old Emily remarked, "I've always wanted to visit Washington to see the White House, the Air and Space Museum and the Capitol, and all the fancy shops. My mom saved money each week from her check just so we could go there over April school vacation." For these children an increase in the family income means an enhanced family life.

Other children find in the two-job income benefits that have nothing to do with material goods; these children understand the relationship between level of income and level of family stress. Many children report that there is less friction in their homes when both parents are working and the household income is increased. In families in which mothers have returned to the work force, youngsters remember how upsetting it was to hear their parents quarrel over money matters. They told us they had worried about losing their house or not having enough money for clothes or to do things with their friends. They were especially concerned that disagreements about money would lead to divorce, since there was so much rancor in the home. Ten-year-old Marie reported, "Before my mom went to work as a bank teller, she and my dad were always arguing about how my mom spent too much. I hated it." The stress that comes from trying to meet heavy financial demands is clearly alleviated in many homes when the mothers seek employment.

Children can understand the role of money without having experienced firsthand the stress of financial problems. Children feel reassured when enough money is available to provide for family needs. In our discussions, some youngsters reasoned that if one parent became unemployed, the other parent would still be providing an income. Eleven-year-old Scott told us, "Recently my father thought he was going to lose his job because they were laying off people where he works. We were all worried about what would happen. At least we knew that my mom had a good job so we wouldn't have to sell our house or anything bad like that." Children who have experienced death or divorce have a clearer sense of the importance of two incomes in a family.

Even younger children have a sense of the role of money in maintaining a certain way of life and meeting the family's needs and responsibilities. Your child is learning from your role as a worker the responsibility as well as the pleasures of earning an income.

Learning about Work

> *My dad's a business consultant and he really likes his job. He's always flying somewhere or other to try to help companies that are having problems.*
>
>   *Chantal, age 9*

Children want to understand what their parents do at work and what the world of work is like. One nine-year-old remarked, "My friend, Hillary, doesn't even know what her mother does at her job. I think that's weird." When you talk about your job, you help your child develop a mental image of how you spend your working hours. Your child can then place you in time and space, rather than wondering where you disappear to every day. In our written survey of fourth through twelfth graders we discovered that 87 percent of the students know what their fathers do for a living, and 83 percent can name their mothers' occupations. Yet between 25 percent and 30 percent cannot describe their parents' jobs.

The youngsters we interviewed are specifically interested in knowing what parents enjoy about their job, what they don't like, and whether or not they like the people they work with. You need to explain your work on your child's level of comprehension. Even at age three and four children can understand explanations like "Mommy teaches children to read and write" or "Daddy fixes cars." By the age of five or six a child can grasp a somewhat fuller description such as "I work with children who have problems with their speech. My job is called a speech therapist. I give them extra help to teach them how to say words correctly."

When children reach the age of eight or nine, they benefit from a more complete discussion of the parents' life at work. Eight-year-old Rebecca commented, "My dad is a lawyer. He explains the cases he's working on and what the different laws say and mean. Sometimes when my brother and I have a fight, my dad has us pretend we are lawyers and we have to present our cases to him."

Most occupations produce their own vocabulary: *input* and *output* for those involved with computers, *inventory* for business people, and so forth. Your child may not feel comfortable stopping you in the middle of a conversation and asking, "What does that mean?" But if you explain the special terminology of your work, your child will better understand what is being discussed around the house and expand her or his knowledge of your job. When you talk about your work, your child learns more than simply the details of a skill or a profession. Your child will listen closely when you talk about significant events of the workday and share amusing anecdotes with them. For through such glimpses of the world of work, children develop an understanding of how you function outside the home. Your reports about your work environment help your child to see you as a competent individual who has knowledge and abilities to contribute to a job.

Explaining work to your child involves discussing problems and difficulties along with accomplishments and satisfactions. Examples of how you cope with job-related pressures and demands made by other adults can teach children to master their own stress. When your child hears stories about how you "kept your cool," you are teaching your youngster effective means of coping with school-related problems. Fourteen-year-old Daria told us, "My dad is a house painter. A couple of weeks ago, he had this job where these people kept changing their minds about what colors to do. He just wanted to get done with their house because he had other work to do. He said he never got angry with them because that wouldn't solve anything." Daria can now appreciate that quick, negative reactions do not produce positive results and can often make matters worse.

When you talk about a mistake you made at work, you show your child that adults are human and fallible. Many children report that they feel more comfortable talking about their own blunders because they know that their parents, too, are occasionally capable of forgetting, misplacing, and procrastinating. Ten-year-old Gabriel recalled, "Once my mother made two hundred copies of the wrong report. She said she felt like crawling in the ground. But she just had to stay late and put together the correct report. I felt easier telling her that I had forgotten my math homework and had to do an extra assignment." You teach your child a valuable lesson when you admit that anyone can be in error. Your child learns to set reasonable standards and to accept mistakes as part of life. As your child pieces together an image of your workday, he or she is able to draw comparisons with the school schedule. Your youngster then begins to see that just as children have rules in school, parents must follow guidelines at work. Elementary school children are particularly fascinated by the discovery that parents must follow restrictions set by employers. Jenny, age eight, said, "My mom works in a department store.

She's on this schedule which says when she can take a break. At least I get a half-hour for recess; my mom's break is only for fifteen minutes."

By the age of seven or eight, children have come to understand some of the aspects of the world of work — the demands and frustrations, the regulations and schedules. In addition, they are learning something even more important — the rewards of satisfying work. When you come home and report a hard day but smile over a job well done despite obstacles, your child hears the gratified tone in your voice and understands that your job makes you happy. As your child listens to you or your friends or relatives talk about your work, she or he is learning about the choices available. As fifteen-year-old Paul explained, "My dad's a cardiologist. He works very hard and sometimes doesn't get home until late at night. But he loves his job and the people he works with. He is challenged by the research he's doing and he makes medicine sound exciting. Even though I know it can be pretty tiring and frustrating, I'd like to be a doctor, too." In Paul's mind, the personal rewards far outweigh the demands or disadvantages of medicine.

Paul's comments are typical of those of many of the youngsters we interviewed. One quarter of the children we interviewed reported that their parents' jobs involve "helping others." Most of these youngsters boast that their parents are responsible for educating other children, for helping people in physical pain, or for counseling the emotionally troubled. Others proudly announce that their parents protect the public by being police officers or firefighters. Susan, a high school senior, related, "My dad teaches history in high school. He likes working with kids, making them think about how events affect their lives. He tries to make his classes exciting. What he probably cares most about is talking to kids about their problems and trying to help them out." Susan, like other children, is pleased that her father has a positive effect on other people's lives. Her pride in her father is a reflection of their satisfaction with his work.

When children are encouraged to learn about the needs of others through listening to their parents talk about their work, they can come to appreciate the role of their parents in the larger world and how that role relates to the parent at home. Sylvia, age ten, remarked, "I think my mom has more patience with me because she's a nurse. She spends her day talking to people and making them feel better. But at night she always takes the time to be with me, to ask about school, and just talk about what's happening." By listening to her mother talk about her work, Sylvia has come to understand the place of compassion and caring in work and at home.

Some children told us that as a result of hearing their parents talk about their work, they have become more aware of stereotyped thinking and have changed their ideas about the handicapped, persons with emotional disorders, or people of different races or socioeconomic backgrounds. Beth, an eighth grader, told us, "My mom works with the mentally retarded. I used to be afraid of those kids in our school and laugh at jokes my friends made about them. Now that my mom talks to me about what she does and what the people can do I try to be nice to these kids in our school. I tell my friends not to say stupid things about them, either." Like this eighth grader, your child can learn compassion and a respect for different people by recognizing that all children do not begin life with equal advantages of health or access to housing, education, and money. Ten-year-old Karen observed, "My dad works for the housing authority in the city. Two weeks ago he took me down to see where they're building a new playground for one of the projects. It doesn't seem fair that where we live there are so many places for kids to play."

By teaching your child about the world of work, he or she will begin to sense the wholeness of work — that it brings satisfaction as well as frustration and requires caring as well as skills. If you expose your child to this part of life, you will be laying the groundwork for the child's healthy career choices in later years. Your child will understand that work can be a positive, integral part of a full life.

Living without Stereotypes

Mothers don't want to be someone else's branch. They want to be their own tree.
Jeff, age 17

Youngsters today have a surprising and gratifying awareness of their parents, both mothers and fathers, as whole people. Children from kindergarten through high school give intelligent and thoughtful reasons for their mothers to be employed beyond the question of money.

Nine-year-old Peter told us, "My mom said she felt like all she was doing all day was housework, and she hates housework." Another child saw his mother's decision to get a job in more poignant terms. Billie, age ten, explained, "When my little brother Tom started first grade, there was no one left at home for my mom to take care of: She felt kind of lonely, so she decided to get a job working at the town library." Youngsters do not fail to notice the change in their mothers when they begin or return to work outside the home. Your child may simply notice that you may seem happier since joining the work force. "Now that my mother is working she's made lots of new friends," an eleven-year-old remarked. Many of these children appreciate the needs of both parents to have jobs that enable them to have contact with others in work-related situations.

Some youngsters intuitively understand one of the most

deeply felt reasons for their mothers' returning to work. Billie's vivid image, quoted above, reveals sensitivity and understanding in this girl. Adolescents, to a much greater degree than younger children, understand their mothers' desire to develop and maintain an identity outside the family. High school students identify their own striving for independence with their mothers' struggles for personal fulfillment. There is little difference in the reaction of female and male adolescents. Both sexes believe that mothers need to experience growth and satisfaction, and both strongly support the idea of their mothers' employment.

Children also see other benefits of having a mother who works outside the home. One teenager commented, "My mother just seems to feel better about herself." Another noted, "My mom doesn't nag me as much about little things because she's so busy. I like it better this way." Those mothers who have feelings of self-assurance and self-worth convey these positive outlooks to their children.

Another powerful result of this social change among mothers is that children now have more positive female role models. Many youngsters see their mothers as intelligent, competent, and proud women who can be both a nurturing parent and a working woman. By watching you grow through your work experience, your child is learning to discard stereotypes and challenge assumptions, and to appreciate your efforts to meet varied responsibilities both at home and on the job.

Your child learns other important lessons and values by watching how you handle work outside the home; many told us that they recognize the advantages of your employment. But your child is also aware of the disadvantages in your employment. You should not be surprised to learn that the negative aspects identified by children in the experience of two-job families relates to the failure of parents to properly balance work and home. Many children do not object to having both parents employed outside the home, but all youngsters object when their parents in one way or another give the appearance of preferring work over family life. Children need a sense of family time after the workday is over. Children describe the loss of family time in four ways, and each reflects how a parent's needs have superseded all other family needs. This chapter considers four questions that can better help you recognize if you are maintaining or losing a proper balance. If you cannot give a firm *no* to each question, you might consider revising your work and family schedules.

Do You Devote Too Much Time to Work?

> *My father works all the time. He leaves the house around 7:00 A.M. and doesn't come home until 8:00 P.M. By then we've all eaten dinner. He eats by himself — sometimes in the kitchen, mostly in front of the TV. He even works at night when he's home.*
> *Kathy, age 14*

Some of the children we interviewed believe that their parents value success on the job more than they value being a good parent. These parents always seem to have something else that "must" be done for work; they either stay late during the week or willingly go in on weekends. Some of these parents are professionals whose energies are devoted to improving their careers. As one high school junior remarked, "Everyone thinks my mom is terrific because she is smart and works hard and is famous. She has time to travel all over the country giving talks. The only person she has no time for is me." Youngsters are not impressed with how famous or competent their parents are on the job if these parents do not spend time with their children at home. If children feel that their concerns and problems only rate second billing they may begin to show signs of stress.

When you come home from work, your child wants your attention to tell you about what happened in class or after school, special weekend plans, or who is going out with whom. Your daughter or son has not seen you for many hours and there is much to talk about. Even if your child is not ready to verbalize every thought, she or he still needs to know that you care enough simply to be near and share your time.

Children feel cheated by actions that clearly place them in second or third place in their parents' schedules. A fourteen-year-old boy stated, "My dad works late almost every night. He acts as if his work is the most important thing in the world." Youngsters want first place at least sometimes, and when they are denied this, they want to know why their time with their parents must always be sacrificed because of work "commitments." Workaholic parents do not endear themselves to their children. These youngsters feel "shut out" of their parents' lives.

Children also resent parents who are at home physically but spend their time working. *Having a parent at home who is still "on the job" is very disheartening for a child.* A parent who is in the house but cannot be disturbed creates a double conflict for children. Youngsters want to play with their father or mother but find they cannot. When they turn to other forms of amusement they may be accused of purposely bothering their parent. The child may not be allowed to practice the piano, use the telephone, or run around being noisy. You want your child to be able to adjust to the special demands of unusual work circumstances, whatever they may be, but you do not want the behavior required by these occasions to become routine. Children at first feel disappointed and then they feel rejected. They don't know how to respond to their parents' distancing behavior. Listen to the phrases these children repeated to us: "Don't bother me," or "Can't you see I'm busy?" or "What do you want now?" Some children just give up trying to gain parental attention after a while because they cannot stand their parents' rejection.

Older children can recognize that a parent who is overly committed to work may make a great employee, but they still consider this parent a terrible mother or father. These youngsters often note the marital discord that develops when one parent focuses primarily on work and neglects the family. One twelve-year-old told us, "Mom just started this new business with her friend. They're working really hard. Now my mom comes home late for dinner a couple of nights a week. I don't think my dad's very happy about it, and neither am I." The tension this youngster is experiencing in her family can be found in many other homes.

Living with a parent who has a total devotion to a job is a sad and frustrating ordeal for a child. Children recognize this as a form of rejection or lack of caring or simply thoughtlessness. Your child may not be angry if occasionally you are forced to work late by your employer. Your child will understand that there are times when you must meet pressing job demands. On some evenings you may be asked to work overtime or fill in on another shift, or to spend extra hours preparing for an important sales meeting, trial, or lecture. Your youngster will adjust to these exceptional circumstances, but your child will also know when you have begun to work "all the time."

What Do You Do After a Hard Day at the Office?

When my dad has had a hard day at work, he takes his anger out on the rest of us. Especially my brother and me. He'll yell at us for the littlest thing, like talking too loud on the

phone. We try staying out of my dad's way as
much as possible until he cools down.
                                        Sandy, age 12

Children resent parents who give of themselves at the
office but stop giving as soon as they are home. These parents may be wonderful listeners on the job, able to em-
pathize with friends and co-workers who are experiencing
hard times, but they are not understanding parents. Always
available to help others, these parents are emotionally
spent by the end of their workday. They are so engrossed
in the activities of work that they do not want to hear about
crises from their youngsters.

A number of parents are unable to leave their work problems at work and to see their children as separate from
those problems. In our research, 37 percent of the children
described their parents as grumpy at the end of the workday. *Most children we spoke with also said they did not*
know how to respond when parents come home from
work in a bad mood. Some children told us they were
afraid that whatever they said would only make an unpleasant situation worse.

When you come home from work, you need to consider
how fair your conduct is toward your child. Long daily absences are especially hard on young children. When you
return home upset, your child's expectations and need for
comfort and attention may go unmet. Further, like you,
your child may have had a bad day. Perhaps your son or
daughter failed a surprise math quiz or had an argument
during recess. Or perhaps your child has waited all day to
tell you some special and exciting news — a good grade
on a history paper or a compliment from a teacher. Your
child needs to talk about what happened, whatever it may
be. But if you focus completely on your feelings and concerns — good or bad — your child will feel cheated.

There are several obvious signs to indicate if your behavior after work has become unfair to your children. In
some homes youngsters become the target of their parents'
wrath when parents are upset by a situation on the job.
Normal child behavior unexpectedly becomes unaccept-
able, and parents lash out verbally or mete out swift pun-
ishments. Suddenly the stereo is too loud, a child is too
boisterous, or spilling a glass of milk is reckless. The parent's anger may begin to seem unpredictable.

Children have a hard time coping not only with their
parents' spoken anger but also with their silent anger.
Parents who think they hold in their feelings usually show
their unhappiness in other ways. Thirteen-year-old Ned
said, "My dad won't talk about what's bothering him. But
you know he's upset. He turns on the TV or reads the news-
paper — and tells us to leave him alone. He just keeps
everything inside." Children are confused when they are
confronted with a silent, seething parent. They don't know
whether they should withdraw to their room or try to talk
to the parent. They look for cues and when they find none,
they feel helpless. Young children cannot be expected to
reason that this anger has nothing to do with them and
should therefore be ignored.

Youngsters cannot be sheltered from all the problems
parents face in the office or at the factory. But some problems are for adults only. Many of the children we interviewed admitted they are scared when they hear their
parents complain about work. Younger children particularly often misinterpret their parents' statements. When
a parent thoughtlessly says he "can't stand his boss" or
"business is slow," the child may take this literally. As
one fourth grader said, "I'm always afraid my mom is going
to lose her job. She comes home yelling or complaining
about something that happened at work. What if her boss
really gets angry and fires her? We need the money. If my

mom loses her job, we won't be able to afford our house." This fear is far too great a burden for a child to bear.

When you are disturbed by something that occurred at work, your children need to be told in terms they can understand that they are not the source of your unhappiness. In this way you relieve your children of the burden of thinking they have done something to cause your displeasure. Betty, age eight, told us, "When my mom comes home in a bad mood she tells us that she's under a lot of pressure at work. She wants us to know she's not angry with us and that even if she yells it's not because we've done anything wrong." Betty's mother has figured out a way to express her anger at parts of her job without injuring her children. Children do not deserve to be used as scapegoats. If you frequently return from work in a terrible mood and treat your children badly, you are straining your relationship with your children and failing to treat them with the fairness they deserve.

Taking out your anger on your child is an obvious sign that your work is overflowing into your home life. But there are other, more subtle signs that should concern you. Almost 90 percent of the children we surveyed reported that their parents sometimes come home after work exhausted. Occasionally you may be so emotionally and physically drained that you simply need peace and quiet. But, when you are exhausted night after night, you are slowly pushing your child out of your life. Some youngsters told us that they no longer ask parents to play games, check homework, watch the Little League game, or go shopping. They do not want to be rejected again. They do not want to hear parents say, "I really can't. I'm too tired." Children feel resentful, hurt, cheated.

Your child needs you at the end of the day, and you can be there if you plan the time right after your arrival. If possible when you first get home, take time to unwind and rejuvenate. Obviously, this is not always possible. If you need to, try to take a break before plunging into the role of mom or dad. A quick shower or a glass of wine may be just the antidote for emotional or physical exhaustion. Or you may prefer a walk, a nap, or a few minutes to read the paper or watch the news. The specific activity is not important. What is important is that you make the effort to restore yourself so you can enjoy your child's company. Adam, age nine, told us, "When my mom's had a hard day at work, she comes home ready to drop. To make herself feel better, she likes to take a long bath. My mom says she feels refreshed after her bath and changing into regular clothes. Then she's ready to make dinner and be with us." The few minutes you take may ensure a far better evening for everyone in the family.

Do Your Stories Bore Your Child?

> *Mom always comes home with stories about*
> *someone from work. She tells us who is*
> *getting a divorce. Or who is having trouble*
> *with their kids. I hate listening to stories*
> *about people I don't even know. Who cares*
> *about their problems? I have my own.*
> *Alison, age 14*

Many youngsters told us that they resent having to listen to the personal problems of other people at work. In some households, dinner conversation is dominated by talk of Mrs. Smith's mother-in-law or Mr. Green's financial problems. When some children compare the amount of time their parents spend discussing the plight of others with the attention they receive, the children feel shortchanged. It is as if their interests and problems do not matter. If you want to relate stories from work, you should only choose incidents that would interest, amuse, or educate your child and omit those that will not. Most anecdotes about work and the people in a company that are relevant to adults have little meaning for children. If you spend every dinner hour talking about the people at work, you are sending your child the message that you are more interested in the people you work with than in your own family.

Youngsters told us how angry they become when their parents compare them to the children of co-workers. Your daughter is not interested in hearing how well the boss's son is doing at school if she is having trouble with history class. And your son may not want to hear that Mrs. Reilly's children willingly help around the house.

Your children want to feel they are special to you. If you find that you often talk about the people at work and not about topics brought up by your children, you are probably becoming too absorbed in the lives of your co-workers. The subjects you choose to discuss at home should be of interest to everyone.

Do You Go Out Too Often on Week Nights?

> It seems like my parents are always out. On Tuesdays they play tennis; Thursdays they have dinner with their friends. And they go out every weekend. I think they'd rather be out than be home with us.
>
> Jimmy, age 12

In addition to working outside the home, some parents go out several nights during the week to attend classes, evening meetings, or exercise groups. They eat out at a restaurant or at the home of friends, play cards or bingo, see a movie or a play. During our interviews children frequently asked us, "Why do my parents have to go out so much?"

Most children feel rejected when their parents continually place their personal needs for relaxation or entertainment above their own needs. Your child wants to enjoy being with you and cannot easily understand why you frequently choose to spend your time with others. To find out if you are going out too often during the week, ask yourself these questions: How often are you at home during the week to have dinner with your children? To check homework assignments? To simply spend a pleasurable evening together as a family? Have you asked your children how they feel about being home without you?

Children are more accepting of a parent's night out when parents show consideration for their children's feelings. First, you should limit the amount of time you are away. If you are usually out more than one evening during the week, you will be absent from your child's life for what feels to a child like a very long time. Second, you should let your child know in advance when you or your spouse will not be coming home. One approach is to mark scheduled nights out on a calendar along with information about where you will be and when you will be home. A calendar will also show you clearly the number of evenings you are absent. If the calendar looks crowded or filled, you know you are going out too often.

Children are more likely to accept one parent's absence if the other parent is present. In fact this situation can be a delightful experience for everyone; when one parent is away, the other has an opportunity to focus on the children and get to know them better. Marva, a fourth grader, commented, "My mom takes a course on Monday nights. So my dad usually takes us out to dinner that night. Sometimes we go for pizza or Chinese food or hamburgers. We have a great time." Marva's family has turned a potentially "lost evening" for the children into a regularly scheduled adventure. Both parents and children are benefiting from this arrangement.

Youngsters also appreciate a few moments with their parents before they go out for the evening. This brief time gives everyone an opportunity to enjoy each other as well as talk with the baby sitter and establish the rules for the night, including homework, television, and bedtime. Some parents provide a special dessert on their nights out. Your child will be especially pleased if you take the time to call and say "good night."

The four questions we have examined relate to the place you give work in your daily life. Most children understand the important role work plays in the lives of their parents, and many accept the need to sacrifice occasionally because of unusual employment demands. But children resent being displaced by a parent's work; they are angry at having their needs relegated to a few hours on a Saturday morning, if they are lucky. And in this, their feelings are an accurate barometer of the place of work in their parents' lives. *If you answered YES to any one of the four questions, or if your child complains that you never have time to be with him or her, you have let your work invade your home and displace your family.* If your child is telling you that she or he feels that all you do is work, you should listen. Learn to come home and "do nothing." Let your child set the pace. The hours you spend at home are equally important for you and your child. Your commitment to protecting these hours should be at least as strong as your commitment to your job.

Chapter 2

How Your Actions Affect Your Child's Self-Esteem

*C*hildren, as well as parents, need and want to feel good about themselves. We all need to believe that we are worthy of others' respect, consideration, and love. With a strong sense of self-esteem we are better able to relate to people around us, and to look upon the present and the future as a challenge we are more capable of meeting. Without a strong sense of self-worth, it would be a struggle to go through each day.

Your child's sense of self-esteem, both positive and negative, develops in large part in response to your words and behavior. Your children see themselves reflected through your eyes. Let us look first at ways your youngster may respond to your conduct, and then how you can further enhance your child's self-esteem.

Determining a Child's Feelings

From the time I was little my parents always made me feel special. They gave me lots of love and made me feel good about myself.

Justin, age 15

A child's sense of self-worth and of being loved or un-loved is shaped by the general pattern of parental behavior. Whether parents are warm and affectionate, accepting but nondemonstrative, or cold and rejecting, their responses play a major part in shaping their child's self-perception. When you freely and openly express affection, your children won't wonder how you feel. They will know they are loved, and this knowledge will make them more self-confident.

To determine how children in our survey felt about themselves, about their relationships with their parents and peers, and about their performance in school, we included a test called the Self-Esteem Inventories. The "inventories," which were developed by Dr. Stanley Coopersmith, measure four kinds of self-esteem: general, home, academic, and social. Coopersmith defines *self-esteem* as "an expression of approval or disapproval, indicating the extent to which a person believes himself or herself competent, successful, and worthy. Self-esteem is a personal judgment of worthiness."

In our survey we also wanted to determine the degree to which parental expressions of love and affection can influence children's positive or negative feelings about themselves and their abilities. According to Dorothy Briggs, author of *Your Child's Self-Esteem*, a high self-esteem comes "from the quality of the relationships that exist between the child and those who play a significant role in his life." The results of our survey also point to a definite statistical link between a high level of self-esteem and a high level of parent contact. Youngsters who report that their parents "often" demonstrate love and affection scored the highest on all four of the Self-Esteem Inventories.

Each inventory consists of a series of statements of certain feelings; youngsters respond by indicating with a checkmark whether the feeling expressed is either "like

me" or "unlike me." Among the statements used to score
general self-esteem (how children feel about themselves)
are: "It's pretty tough to be me," "I have a low opinion
of myself," "I can usually take care of myself," and "I'm
pretty happy." Of the children who showed low general
self-esteem, 60 percent had low parent contact compared
to youngsters with high general self-esteem, 53 percent of
whom had high parent contact.

Unlike children with high general self-esteem, those
with low general self-esteem are unhappy with themselves.
These youngsters may wish to be older or younger than
they are, to be of the opposite sex, or to have a different
physical appearance. They do not believe they are worthy
and capable, and they may show their discontent by either
shy or aggressive behavior. Although they need praise and
acceptance, their actions may prevent them from receiving
the approval they crave. Unfortunately, as our survey revealed, parents of these children are more likely to offer
criticism or — even worse — to show indifference to their
children's plight than to give them the praise and affection they need.

Youngsters with high general self-esteem seem content
with life's offerings. They genuinely like themselves, not
in a conceited or smug way, but with an inner assuredness.
These children generally feel in control of their lives rather
than at the mercy of circumstances. They are able to accept
challenges and to bounce back from defeat. Because they
are happy and fun to be around, they attract people who
reinforce their sense of well-being. As we might expect,
these children — according to our survey — more often
than not have parents who provide the love and praise that
help them to maintain their emotional equilibrium.

Among the statements used to score *home self-esteem*
(how children feel in relation to their parents) are: "My
parents expect too much of me," "My parents understand

me," "My parents and I have a lot of fun together," and "No one pays much attention to me at home." Of the youngsters with the lowest scores in home self-esteem, 60 percent had low parent contact; 61 percent of those with high home self-esteem reported high parent contact.

These scores suggest that youngsters with low home self-esteem are not receiving enough emotional support and sustenance to make them feel good about their place in the home. Their parents may be spending too much time at work or bringing work home too often. They may be too tired after work to relate to their youngsters in a thoughtful manner, or they may spend little time in pleasant conversation. Some of these parents may be expecting a mature behavior beyond the capability of their youngsters — requiring them to stay home alone at too young an age for too long a period of time or demanding that they care for younger siblings. Or the parents may simply be neglecting or ignoring the needs of their youngsters.

Low home self-esteem may also indicate troubled relationships between these youngsters and their parents. Parents may unintentionally develop a pattern of parent-child behavior that reinforces a youngster's unfavorable opinion of himself or herself. Parents may act in a withdrawn or overly demanding manner that only underlines their youngster's sense of inferiority and being unloved. The children with low home self-esteem were most likely to agree with the statement, "There are many times I'd like to leave home."

Youngsters with high home self-esteem have parents who enjoy being with them and spend time on family activities that promote closeness and harmony. Their parents are willing to focus their attention on their youngsters in a caring way, to nurture them, and to provide acceptance and love.

The inventory measures *academic self-esteem* by statements like these: "I find it very hard to talk in front of the class," "I often get discouraged in school," "I'm proud of my schoolwork," and "I'm doing the best work I can." Of the youngsters who revealed low academic self-esteem, 62 percent had low parent contact. By comparison, 58 percent of the youngsters with high academic self-esteem had high parent contact.

School personnel are quick to point out that without parental encouragement and assistance it is much more difficult for youngsters to achieve academically. Most children want their parents to be involved to some degree with their education and when they cannot get their parents interested in their schoolwork, they may begin to question their abilities. By contrast, children who know that their parents care about their work while still being realistic about their capabilities are most likely to succeed in school.

Finally, the test measures children's *social self-esteem* (how they feel about their relationships with peers) through statements like these: "I'm popular with kids my own age," "Kids usually follow my ideas," "I don't like to be with other people," and "Kids pick on me very often." Of the students who had low social self-esteem 54 percent also had low parent contact. Of those with high social self-esteem, 59 percent reported high parent contact.

Children with low social self-esteem usually feel others do not like them. These youngsters may be uncomfortable around their peers and unsure of how to behave. Somehow, they just don't seem to "fit in." They are usually the last ones chosen for the baseball game or the ones for whom the teacher has to assign partners for team projects because no one asks to work with them. These youngsters agreed most often with the statement, "I don't like to be with other people."

Youngsters with high social self-esteem often serve as

magnets for their peers. They are fun to be around, get along well with children in various age ranges, and can gather a group together for play or to "hang out." They accept other children's strengths and do not try to exploit their weaknesses. Because of this thoughtfulness, they are trusted and well liked.

The strong correlation we found between high self-esteem in each category and high parent contact led us to examine more closely the relation between high self-esteem and the amount of time children spent at home alone after school. To understand this relationship better, we separately analyzed the responses of youngsters aged thirteen and younger. The findings are dismaying. Children who were home alone for two hours or more scored lowest of all children in all age groups on three of the four inventories: general, academic, and home self-esteem; they scored second lowest on social self-esteem.

The youngsters with the lowest self-esteem were those who were left at home alone for the longest time and who received the least amount of parental — especially father — nurture. For these children, being home alone for two hours or more exacerbates their feelings of inadequacy. They are forced to deal with a situation that is overwhelming for them — caring for themselves for long periods of time each day without proper supervision or emotional support. They are not prepared to cope with their fears and loneliness; indeed, even few adults could survive an environment in which they received as little moral support. The home self-esteem ratings for these children were significantly lower than those of their peers, indicating that these youngsters have little confidence in their relationship to their parents.

When we considered separately the scores of adolescents, we again found a strong correlation between low parent contact and low ratings on the Self-Esteem Inventories. In fact, the older youngsters' self-esteem ratings showed an even greater link between parental behavior and the child's self-esteem than the ratings of younger children. The results suggest strongly that parents cannot assume that because adolescents look and act like adults, they no longer need warmth, security, and praise. They need these reinforcements just as their younger siblings do. Adolescents are going through an especially difficult time; they are adjusting to inner changes and outside pressures, and they need their parents' guidance and support. Even though adolescence may be a stressful time for parents, it is a far more stressful time for adolescents. The results of our surveys emphasize the importance of this period for building high self-esteem.

Building Your Child's Self-Esteem

My mom cares how I do in school, but she cares even more about how I feel about school — whether I think I'm doing well or not.
                                        Rebecca, age 11

The survey results outlined above leave no doubt about the role of the parents in the development of the child's self-esteem. In many instances your child's self-esteem does not depend on what you say specifically but rather on the evidence of your concern. A simple show of interest can tell your child that he or she is worthwhile in your eyes, and that is the measure that counts most.

The clear message we received in our interviews is that adolescents who like themselves have parents who like them — and let them know it. Sadly, the opposite is also true. As one adolescent complained to us, "If my parents treated their friends the way they treat me, they'd have no friends." Such a powerful statement requires attention. You treat your friends with thoughtfulness and respect, and your children deserve at the very least the same consideration. Once you become aware of how your actions affect your child's feelings, you can better avoid the extremes that lead to low self-esteem. According to Coopersmith, there are "indirect indications that domination, rejection, and severe punishment of children result in lowered self-esteem. Under such conditions they have *fewer experiences of love and success* and tend to become generally submissive and withdrawn, although occasionally veering to the opposite extreme of aggression and domination" (emphasis added).

According to the children's written questionnaires, fathers play a significant role in their youngsters' development of self-esteem. The impact of strong father contact on a youngster's self-esteem seems to be greater than that of strong mother contact. This may be in part because children say they know they can count on their mothers to be fairly consistent in showing affection and responding to their needs, whereas fathers' behavior is less predictable. Among the youngsters' responses of all ages, 60 percent of those with low father contact have low home self-esteem, whereas 62 percent of those with high father contact have high home self-esteem. A similar pattern is found in the results on academic self-esteem. Of youngsters with low father contact, 60 percent scored low on academic self-esteem in contrast to their peers with high father contact, 58 percent of whom scored high on academic self-esteem.

Expressions of affection are an important means of helping children feel good about themselves, but determining if you are showing enough affection or not enough may be difficult. To learn the degree of physical and verbal affection that children of working parents receive, we used the Hollander Parent Contact Scale, together with other supplementary material. We called this exercise *How My Parents Act Questionnaire*. It consisted of sixteen statements, including "kissed me goodbye when I left them or they left me," "hugged or embraced me," "told me they loved me." Children circled "hardly ever," "sometimes," or "often" as a choice of response for each parent. Youngsters responded separately on how they perceived their mothers' and fathers' everyday behavior toward them. The test allowed us to determine variations depending on how long children were left home alone and to compare the responses of youngsters according to age group and gender.

Children of both sexes and all ages clearly feel that their mothers consistently demonstrate a greater amount of love and affection than do their fathers. The overwhelming conclusion to be drawn from the questionnaires is that mothers are much more physically and verbally expressive than fathers. This finding was strongly confirmed in our oral interviews with youngsters. Fifteen-year-old Charlene told us, "Mothers seem to know that kids need lots of loving; fathers still have to learn that." In general, children feel less close to their fathers than from their mothers. Several adolescents remarked, "It's hard to get close to my father. He's not a very warm person."

The differences between the attitudes of mothers and fathers is most apparent in the children's responses regarding their parents' nonverbal displays of affection. For children age thirteen and under, only 40 percent of fathers but 60 percent of mothers often "hug or embrace" their children. One fourth of the fathers but only one tenth of the mothers hardly ever "hug or embrace" their youngsters. Of the children who are at home alone the longest — two hours or more each day — one in three reports *hardly ever* being embraced by their fathers. An eleven-year-old told us, "I can't remember the last time my father actually hugged me."

Adolescents, age thirteen and older, fare even less well than younger children. Fewer than half of mothers and one third of fathers embrace their older children with some degree of frequency. Fathers make an even further distinction and are twice as likely to embrace their daughters as their sons. Luke, age twelve, observed, "It's sad when I think my own father doesn't like to hug me very much. He makes me feel rejected."

The results are even worse for parents kissing their children other than to say "good night" or when they leave one another. Almost one father in four and one mother in eight hardly ever kisses their youngsters age thirteen and younger except on those particular occasions. Forty percent of fathers and just over half of mothers often kiss these youngsters. We were delighted when ten-year-old Katie beamed, "When my mom and dad come home from work they give me lots of hugs and kisses because they're so happy to see me." At the other extreme, children in this age group who are home alone the longest are least often kissed by their parents: fewer than one fourth of the fathers and 40 percent of the mothers often kiss these youngsters.

A hug, kiss, squeeze, or pat on the back communicates affection. Many children want and need both parents to be more physically demonstrative. Unfortunately, our society discourages men from being physically expressive, particularly toward their male children. Fathers are thus often reluctant to express themselves in this manner. In general, fathers begin to pull away from their children at an early age, and by preadolescence there is a marked decrease in the physical expression of affection. One thirteen-year-old boy told us, "When I was seven my dad told me it wasn't manly to kiss anymore. That was it." By this failure to communicate love through physical contact, fathers are defining a pattern of behavior that their sons may follow in their future families. The opportunity for fathers to be a warm role model is being wasted.

Children definitely feel the loss of a father's affection. Our survey indicates that the youngsters who are at the greatest disadvantage are those thirteen and younger who spend two hours or more alone at home each day. It is distressing to realize that some working parents who expect their children to care for themselves after school do not make a greater effort to be emotionally close to their children when they are together.

At the other end of the scale are children who are at home alone less than one hour each day; these children receive the greatest amount of physical affection from their parents. Rachel, a ten-year-old in this group, related, "My dad tells us that after his hard day at work he can't wait to come home to his family. When he walks in the door he expects my sister and me to stop what we are doing to greet him so he can say 'hello,' ask about our day, and give us a hug. It may sound funny, but I like it."

The simplest but most powerful means of showing affection is by saying, "I love you." In our research we found that seven fathers in eight, but nineteen mothers in twenty, frequently tell their youngsters age thirteen and younger that they love them. But for the children in this age group who are home alone the longest, only one father in five shows affection this way. Further, 20 percent of fathers and 10 percent of mothers *hardly ever* tell their adolescents that they love them. Sixteen-year-old Michelle straightforwardly told us, "How come if my parents really care about me they never tell me?" Michelle really touches on the crux of the matter for many parents. If you have become so absorbed in other areas of your life that you have forgotten that there are people in your home that you care about, you need to take time to think about what you are doing and what you are not saying.

Fortunately, children like Michelle are not the norm. Over 60 percent of fathers and 75 percent of mothers often said "I love you" to their children under age fourteen. Almost two thirds of mothers of adolescents often said, "I love you." But only half of the youngsters who are at home alone for two hours or more and only half of the adolescents report that their fathers are verbally expressive in an affectionate way.

Throughout our discussions with youngsters we repeatedly encountered the same theme: *The longer a child is at home alone, the less likely is the parent to convey love for the child and the more likely is the child to have low self-esteem.* Your child needs to know you care. If you cannot be home in the afternoon when school is out, you can find other moments to express your love for your child. You can build your child's self-esteem by small, simple acts that remind both you and your child of the bond between you. You can hug or kiss your child during a pleasant evening talk or after finishing a household chore. If you are not comfortable with physical demonstrations of affection, you can still strengthen attachments by verbal expressions of warmth and caring. Your child will benefit enormously when you make a daily, conscious effort to show your love — before leaving for work; by putting notes in your child's lunch; in telephone calls from work; upon returning home from work; during dinner; and before bed.

No matter how busy you are, you should try to act in a way that promotes your child's self-worth. The following is a list of basic rules of conduct that will help you build higher self-esteem in your child.

- Act in a loving, caring manner.
- Create an emotionally supportive household environment.
- Voice delight at just being your children's parent.
- Tell your children that they are special and cherished.

- Show acceptance for your children's limitations as well as strengths.
- Offer praise freely but sincerely.
- Treat your children with respect.

Chapter 3

Communicating with Your Child

Youngsters *in homes in which* mothers and fathers both work may have fewer opportunities to communicate with their parents. This can be a dilemma for parents and children. Yet there are many solutions. Most children love to talk — to explore ideas and sort out experiences. They need to share their feelings about growing up and hear you relate your knowledge and insights. But to communicate with your child, you must first be willing to listen.

Listening to Your Child

> *If parents want to have a good relationship with their kids they've got to be prepared to talk with them. Some of my friends' parents are so busy with their own lives they seem to forget how much their kids need them. My mother and father have always let me know that they're ready to listen whenever I want to talk.*
>
> Linda, age 17

We live in an age of the wonders of communication technology, yet some parents and children find it harder and harder to talk to each other. Youngsters often complained to us that they cannot even attract their parents' attention. One youngster commented, "My dad likes to read the paper and talk to me at the same time. Well, it just doesn't work." Another said, "How are you supposed to talk to your parents if they're always watching television?" Not many adults would tolerate this type of situation, and children resent being given only half a person's attention.

Children who feel let down when parents divide their attention between listening to them and engaging in other activities may turn to a friend or relative when they want to talk about something important. Still others may feel they have no one to listen to them.

Over half of the children aged thirteen and under who are at home alone for more than two hours reported that their fathers hardly ever respond positively to their need to talk. The children's hurt and disappointment are obvious in their descriptions of their home life. Twelve-year-old Patrick reported, "My father doesn't get home until 5:30 P.M. My mother comes home even later. I really want to tell my dad what's happened during the day, but he just doesn't listen." Many of the youngsters clearly feel rejected. After being without adult or sometimes any companionship for at least two hours, they need a parent to listen to them — to hear about their day and to learn about their feelings.

Children who are at home alone for the longest period of time, and therefore in greatest need of verbal support and an opportunity to talk with others, are least likely to receive that support from their fathers. Children who are at home alone less than two hours as well as adolescents among the other group receive slightly more of their fathers' attention. Sixty percent of these youngsters are able to get their fathers to listen to them when something important is involved.

Overall children gave mothers higher ratings in their ability to listen. We heard again and again that after work, mothers make a greater effort to listen to their children than do fathers. Almost two thirds of those aged thirteen and under who were at home alone for more than two hours reported that their mother often "listens to me when I need to talk about something important." Almost three quarters of the youngsters who are home alone less than two hours expressed this view. Again, we were disturbed to find that those children who are without adult supervision the most receive the least "listening" time.

The children interviewed are equally clear about what they want to talk about. *Children of all ages emphasize that they want to talk about feelings.* Youngsters especially want to be able to tell their parents when they are afraid — of being home alone, of having something happen to them or to their parents, of having too much responsibility, or of failing in school. But often they sense that parents don't want to be told about these concerns. One eighth grader remarked, "When I try to talk to my dad about something he doesn't want to hear, he says he has work to do." This father is not only preventing his child from working out a problem together but also teaching him to avoid asking his father difficult questions or topics.

Children are especially sensitive to a parent's effort to evade certain topics. Many children told us that parents frequently brush aside conversations on sensitive subjects. Nevertheless, children need to ask these questions, share their ideas, and hear their parents' thoughts on such personal matters as sexuality (the issue youngsters say parents most avoid), drugs, God, religion, and death. No child should be burdened by a fear or worry simply because a parent finds the subject uncomfortable or embarrassing. A few moments listening to your youngster and answering questions can make an enormous difference in your child's security. One sixth grader worries every day because her parents won't talk to her openly: "I have this dog, Patches, who is pretty old but I love her. She's great company in the afternoon when I'm home by myself. I'm really afraid of coming home one day and finding her dead. I know if I told my parents how I feel they'd just say, 'Don't worry, nothing will happen to her.' How do they know? I do worry." A brief conversation could remove this child's fear.

Parents are sometimes reluctant to talk about relationships within the family. In our written survey, one child in five reported that their fathers rarely talk with them about "important family matters." For mothers, the figure is one in ten. Only 40 percent of fathers and 50 percent of mothers speak with their children about significant family issues. Some youngsters want to talk about difficulties with their older siblings who are in charge of them after school and are too bossy, pay little attention to them, or even physically mistreat them. Older youngsters may need to discuss the pressures they feel when they are in charge of the house and also must do their schoolwork. Some children also told us they need to talk about their relationship and their parents' relationships with grandparents (especially those living in the household).

Regardless of the subject they want to talk about, children resent being ignored, shunted aside, cut off, or interrupted when they are describing an experience or feeling that is important to them. Youngsters crave *undistracted parental time*, time when parents' entire attention is focused on their children. They react with delight when they know that they are a most important part of their parents' lives.

Undistracted time frees you and your child to talk. When you consciously decide to slow down and listen closely to your youngsters and share ideas with them, your children will more likely respond with the same openness and sharing. Fourteen-year-old Lorin's comment reveals how important a simple conversation can be to a child: "My mom and I have our best talks late at night. It's the one time mom can finally relax. She's ready to hear what's happening with me and tell me about her day. I like these times the best. They make me feel close to her."

When you give your children the opportunity to discuss their feelings, you are giving them permission to voice their fears and anxieties, to ask questions, and to seek support and guidance. This is a very simple way by which you can strengthen your relationship with your children. By allowing undistracted time for conversation, you give your youngsters individual attention and show consideration for their feelings, respect for their ideas, and interest in being actively involved in their lives.

To discover how much undistracted time you devote to each child, it might be helpful to keep a one-week chart. At the end of each evening, record the number of times you interrupted a conversation with a child to do something else or tried carrying on a discussion while your mind was focused elsewhere. You may discover that the telephone or television interferes with conversation to a greater extent than you realized or that you take work home as a way to avoid discussions. The chart will also show you if one child is receiving more attention than another — an imbalance that needs correcting.

Below is a list we compiled based on the complaints youngsters made most frequently during our interviews. Following these basic rules will enable your child to feel that you do indeed want to listen. Some ways to encourage communication are to:

- Willingly stop other activities to talk with your youngster.
- Set aside time for each child.

- Focus attention on your child's words, tone of voice, and body language.
- Allow your child to choose the topic of discussion.
- Let your child have an opportunity to dominate the discussion.
- Express understanding and sympathy.
- Respect your youngster's point of view and don't evaluate feelings or opinions.
- Maintain eye contact.
- Sit physically close to your youngster.
- Relax and enjoy the conversation.

Criticizing Your Children

If I get a B on a paper, my father wants to know how many kids got an A and why I wasn't one of them.

Mark, age 16

Parents who rarely make time for conversation with their children still find time to criticize. If this is the only kind of discussion children have with their parents, the bond between parent and child can be irreparably damaged. Youngsters do not know how to respond to a parent's verbal assaults. Many "shrink a little inside." Others daydream to escape. A few attempt to answer the unfair charges, which only leads, as one fifteen-year-old described, "to a yelling match, with me always losing." Conversation punctuated by criticism or orders is not conversation at all, but a fencing match. And it is a match in which one participant, the child, is wearing no protection; the child is defenseless and easily hurt. There is no winner in such a contest. Parents should avoid falling into a pattern of behavior that can only injure their children. Children complain in particular about criticism that is unfair, embarrassing, or rude. Let us look at each of these more closely. Children resent it when parents begin a conversation with "You never..." This kind of sweeping statement is unfair and only leads to further accusations and recriminations. Similarly, youngsters also hate sentences that begin with phrases like "You always forget..." Just as no one is flawless, so no one is consistently imperfect. You deny your child's good points and good behavior when you focus only on the negative. You should be especially aware of this when you first arrive home from work. Your opening comments should not sound as if you are on the attack. A negative remark when you first enter the house can set a discordant tone for an entire evening.

Children should never be humiliated or embarrassed in front of school friends, siblings, or adults. If you use belittling language, you strike at the heart of your relationship with your youngster. By resorting to this type of behavior, for whatever reasons, you are breaking what all children think of as an unwritten rule: *Parents should not say anything that causes their children to lose face with others.* Children say they are sad and angry at this sort of behavior, but the damage to self-esteem can be great. And as one twelve-year-old observed, "My dad can be really nasty when something goes wrong at his job. He starts calling me names like 'fatso' or 'chubby' even in front of my friends, especially if I'm eating ice cream. It really hurts."

If your child needs to be reprimanded, you should do this in private. And even then, your statements should enable your child to maintain a sense of dignity. Above all, you should not use your child as a target when you are frustrated at work or in some other area of your life.

Youngsters are also sensitive to the tone of voice adults use, particularly their parents. Your way of asking your child to carry out a chore or an errand tells your child how much respect you feel for her or his assistance. Children dislike being addressed as if they were mechanical objects. Children want parents to talk to them in a polite, thoughtful manner — to say "please" and "thank you." And they want to be treated with the same respect their parents receive from their co-workers.

Youngsters told us that unless there is a pressing reason why something should be taken care of immediately, they should not be expected to jump at commands. They resent the implication that whatever a parent wants is always more important than what they may be doing at the moment. Some children made the sensible suggestion that parents should ask for tasks to be completed within a certain period of time. This allows the child time to do the task and lessens the chance for an argument.

To determine whether you have fallen into a pattern that blocks discussion and creates ill will, consider each of the factors listed below. As you read through the list, remember the times you criticized your child. Listen especially to the tone of your voice. Specifically, you should make mental or written notes on how often you:

- Speak to your youngster in a harsh manner.
- Criticize your child's words, behavior, or appearance.
- Embarrass your child.
- Issue commands.

By observing the effects of your words and actions on your children and by changing the manner and tone of your speech, you can better talk to your child about chores or deadlines or any other subject without alienating your child or creating disharmony in the home.

Telephoning Your Child

When I get home at 3:20, the first thing I do is make a snack and wait for my mom to

call. She likes to call to make sure I'm okay.
I usually have a lot to tell her about school,
how much homework I have, who is coming
over. I wouldn't want to wait until she came
home from work to speak to her. I'd probably
forget half the things I want to tell her.
Besides, I feel better after hearing her voice.
                                              Richard, age 11

The telephone can be an important tool for families with
two working parents; it can do far more than reassure you
about your child's safety. Indeed, youngsters from fourth
grade through high school emphatically want daily telephone contact with their parents during working hours.
Yet our written survey surprisingly revealed that only 54
percent of mothers and only 36 percent of fathers sometimes call home from work. The survey results for children age thirteen and younger are even more disturbing.
Fewer than half of the youngsters who are at home alone
for two hours or more receive phone calls from their
mothers, and fewer than one third are called by their
fathers. Children who are alone for two hours or less fare
better: 60 percent said their mothers sometimes call, and
45 percent said their fathers sometimes do. We discovered
in the personal interviews that the telephone calls many
children receive are often made by both their mothers and
fathers. In other words, there are even fewer total contacts
than the above statistics suggest.

Your children need to know that you continue to care
about them when you are at work. Calling home is a way
of letting your youngsters know that you are thinking of
them even though you cannot be with them. Further, the
rewards of a brief conversation can be great for both parent
and child. Twelve-year-old José told us, "My dad calls me
a couple of times a week. He asks how practice went and

tells me not to watch too much TV. He usually can only talk a few minutes, but that means a lot to me." This father listens to what his son wants to talk about and then gives a quick word on television. Both understand that the other cares.

The afternoon telephone call fulfills an important emotional function. After a long day, your child wants to talk about what happened. Your youngsters enjoy sharing news of what took place in school: the B+ they scored on the science test or the invitation they received for a party on Saturday night. They will especially need to speak with you when they have had a difficult or upsetting day at school: when they were chosen last to play volleyball at gym or when the teacher yelled at them for talking too much. Children long for a sympathetic listener who will share their excitement as well as their problems and pain at the end of the day.

In addition, the telephone call will ease the transition from a crowded school to an empty house. By welcoming your child home with a phone call, you will alleviate some of the anxiety your child feels about being home alone. A major theme that flows through the writing of the children is feeling lonely and scared when they are home unsupervised. Not only were these feelings mentioned in over 50 percent of the written stories but they quickly surfaced as major concerns of the children we interviewed. Even though you think your child is safe, you should still take the time to help your child over these fears. The comforting effect of a phone call was described by Jessica, age twelve, who told us, "This may sound weird, but sometimes I sit by the phone and say, 'Please ring. Come on, mom or dad.' I say it over and over to myself. When the phone rings I feel happy and relieved. My wish came true."

Telephoning home from work can also serve a variety of practical purposes. A regular call in the afternoon can keep everyone in the family up-to-date. You should use this time to tell your children about any changes in your schedule that will alter the time you arrive home. Your phone call can help your children with instructions about homework or starting dinner. Or you can simply remind them to lock the door and then reassure them of their safety. Best of all, use the call to express feelings of warmth and closeness. Your children will never tire of hearing you say, "I love you" or "I called because I miss you." However long or short your call is, create as pleasant a conversation as possible. Try to focus on the positive. Remember that your youngsters look forward to this call and your tone of voice is as important as what you say. Youngsters do not want parents engaging in a monologue.

The practical arrangements for making or receiving daily telephone calls should be clear both to you and your children. Both parents may not be able to assume equal responsibility for phoning home; one parent may have easier access to a telephone in the afternoon. Or one may have a busier schedule than the other between 3:00 and 4:00 P.M. when the children arrive home from school. Some parents may want to alternate the responsibility, each parent taking a week at a time. Some parents prefer to have their children call their place of work. Many children told us how they enjoyed coming home, dialing the telephone, and hearing a parent on the other end. Some children even practiced their conversations with the parents "in their heads" before they actually made their call.

In view of youngsters' feelings about telephoning, we were disturbed that only three quarters of the children in our survey know their mother's work phone number. Fewer know their father's work number. Children age thirteen and younger who were at home alone for two hours or more each day were most likely to know the parents' work phone numbers. More than nine out of ten of these children had their mother's work number, and eight in ten had their father's.

By the time your children are in the fourth grade, they should have memorized one — and preferably both — of their parents' work numbers. Information increases your child's safety. Some children in our survey have no way of getting in touch with a parent in case of an emergency. This is a burden of worry no child should have to carry.

You should write down your telephone numbers and post them where your children can always find them. The refrigerator door and a bulletin board in the kitchen are favorite spots. You may also want your child to carry the numbers in a wallet or jacket.

In addition, give your children clear, explicit guidelines on the frequency of calls to your place of business. According to our interviews, mothers are more willing to be interrupted by their youngsters' calls than are fathers. This indicates that fathers need to take on greater responsibility for their children home alone. Your youngsters should know which parent can more readily accommodate interruptions and which parent is more receptive to spontaneous calls. If you have a job that makes regular telephone calls difficult, you should identify another adult your children can phone after school. A grandparent or a close friend may be happy to hear from your children.

Every child wants to believe that someone cares enough to listen, to agree, to sympathize, to care. Your youngster turns to you to share his or her deepest longings or more troubling fears. If you have learned to listen, your child is more likely to want to talk with you and also listen to you.

Chapter 4

Creating Time to Be Together

*F*amilies in which both parents work face heavy demands on their time. Many children told us they need to be with their parents more often, just to relax and have fun. When your child begins to feel this way, draw back and look at the time you do have and how you can use it to enhance your relationship. Your son or daughter does not necessarily want a weekend at a resort on the coast or in the mountains, but undistracted time to be with you — to enjoy being your child. You already have time in your schedule to spend with your child, but you may not know how to use it well. Below are several suggestions on how to find and utilize time to create greater family happiness.

Dinner Time

The only time we're together as a family is for dinner. Then we really get to hear what everyone's doing. We're all pretty talkative and all want to be heard. We can also be competitive to see who gets to speak first.

*My sister, Ronnie, usually wins because she's
the youngest and doesn't have much patience.
She likes to tell us what happened in first
grade, what book she's reading and what she
did at her after-school program. It's fun listening to her. My mom and dad just like to
find out how our day went, what we did,
how we are.*

Judi, age 12

Many children told us that dinner time is the one occa-
sion when all family members are present. It is the only
time when they can experience their family as a unit and
not as a group of individual players. This coming together
reinforces children's sense of closeness and belonging, and
offers them the special joy of feeling the warmth of family
members taking pleasure in each other's company.

Some children report that they hardly ever eat together
as a family, or that they eat together only a few nights a
week because their parents work late or attend evening
meetings. Youngsters understand that it may be difficult
for their parents to be home for dinner every evening, but
on less busy nights they want their parents to come home
and join them for supper. If your children know that you
are making an effort to be at home as often as possible for
dinner, they will feel more satisfied. Ten-year-old Juanita
told us, "My dad has to work late twice a week. But he's
always home on Tuesday, Thursday, and Sunday so we can
eat together."

Dinner can be one of the best sharing times for a parent.
By encouraging conversation, you will learn about your
children's day and experience their world. Use this time
to help your children work out solutions to problems at
school or with friends or to check on how they are spending
their time. Or you can simply let your children know how

delighted you are to be with them and tell them that you love them. You should compliment them on how well they handle their responsibilities after school. This is also the perfect time to make weekend plans. Your children probably would also like to hear about your day. Listening to you talk about what you accomplished or about a problem you encountered will help them to gain an understanding of what you do.

In some households lively political conversation dominates the dinner table. Fifteen-year-old Josh explained, "My mom and dad like us to be aware of what's happening in the world, so we usually have these pretty interesting talks at dinner. My brother and I also bring up any issue we want. Some of my friends wish their parents would have such open discussions at their house." As Josh's comment indicates, children are not necessarily interested in any particular topic but rather in the opportunity to talk openly with their parents.

Once you realize how important dinner time can be for your family, you may want to alter your evening arrangements to give more time to your family in some way during the dinner period. Not all children can wait for dinner until both parents come home; younger children, in particular, may become irritable if not fed at an early hour. Nevertheless, families have worked out various solutions to this problem. Some youngsters have a late snack, around five o'clock, to tide them over. Nine-year-old Joel reported another solution: "I get too hungry most nights to wait to have supper with my parents. But I save my dessert and eat my ice cream with them when they have supper."

In most homes with two working parents, the entire burden of preparing dinner still falls on working mothers. Fortunately, in other families, meal preparation has become a joint family venture in order to ensure time together. In thirteen-year-old Damien's home the division of labor among the children draws in everyone: "Each of the kids in our house has a job to do. One of us sets and clears the table, one of us makes the salad or peels the vegetables, and one of us brings over all the drinks and extra stuff like ketchup or salt. We rotate our jobs each week, because none of us likes to clean up and my brother Sam and I both like to do the salad — because that's fun."

You can build a feeling of family togetherness by encouraging your youngsters to take part in dinner preparation. Tasks should be assigned according to your children's age and ability — not according to their sex. No one should always get stuck with the "dirty jobs." As much as possible children should be given "fun jobs," like pouring milk or fruit juice. Again rotate the chores or let each child have a day off occasionally.

Even though adolescents may be capable of preparing the entire dinner, you must be careful not to take advantage of these youngsters. Older children do not want to be rewarded for their competency by being asked to do even more work. *And expecting adult behavior and responsibility from people who are still children can have adverse emotional consequences.* One thirteen-year-old sadly summarized how some youngsters feel: "I sometimes wish that someone would be home and surprise me. Cook supper for me instead of my cooking for myself." It's no fun to eat alone, and it's not fair to the child.

The precautions you take to ensure that everyone participates equally in the preparation should be extended to the dinner hour itself. By establishing basic rules of conduct for parents and children, dinner can be a more pleasant and satisfying meal. Children told us how disturbing and disappointing it is when dinner becomes a time of friction. Youngsters report that conflict often arises over friends, chores, homework, and the use of the telephone. If certain topics always cause arguments at dinner, set as your first rule the exclusion of these specific topics from discussion at the supper table.

A common cause of upheaval is sibling rivalry. Youngsters readily admit that they often compete with their sisters and brothers to be the first to talk or be the one who speaks the longest at the dinner table. Each child wants the spotlight. During our interviews, many youngsters suggested that each child take turns being the first one to speak. This is sensible and fair.

A telephone call can also be a major disruption to dinner conversation. You and your children could agree not to accept calls at suppertime under ordinary circumstances. Seventeen-year-old Philip's family follows this rule: "If the phone rings we are not allowed to talk. We have to tell our friends to call back. My parents don't talk on the phone either. They feel that dinner time is for all of us. Most of my friends know this so they don't call while we're eating." This type of rule permits the focus of attention to remain where it should be — on the family.

The same decision to make dinner time special for the entire family can be extended to evenings when the family eats out. For many children there is a special pleasure in eating out with their parents. They feel like they have their parents' complete attention. No one need be concerned over who is responsible for pouring the milk or for washing the dishes later. Moreover, it is not even necessary to have both parents present. Having one parent all to themselves can be a treat for many children. By taking one child out to eat — whether it is for breakfast on Saturday morning or pizza on Tuesday night — you create a special time for closeness with that child. Rhodie, an eighth grader, told us, "Every other Wednesday night my dad takes me out to dinner. My dad works late a lot so I don't get to see him as much as I'd like, but it's great going out with him, having him all to myself — without anyone interrupting us."

Both you and your children will benefit by breaking the daily routine and taking time for yourselves.

Bedtime

The only good part about going to bed is that I get to talk to my mom — with no one bothering us. It's our special time together. We talk about my friends, what's happening in school, what we're doing for the weekend.
                                                    Roanne, age 11

For many children, bedtime represents time alone with a parent — having mom or dad all to themselves. It may be the one moment during the entire day when they do not have to share a parent with their siblings or with the other parent. For many children, this makes bedtime extra special. Nine-year-old Lori exclaimed, "My brothers aren't allowed to bother my mom when she's putting me to bed. They're supposed to LEAVE US ALONE!"

When both parents work, they may be too tired to carry on the usual bedtime routine, forgetting how important this part of the day can be for children. A number of youngsters complained to us that what used to be a regular time for closeness and sharing is now more sporadic. One boy remarked, "My parents used to take turns putting me to bed, now they tell my older brother to read to me." These parents are being unfair to both children. Not surprisingly, many youngsters are angry at the chronic excuses of parents. They are too tired, too busy, or too distracted.

If you find that you are regularly missing your child's bedtime regardless of the reasons, it is time to reassess your schedule. Putting your child to bed does take time, but this is time well spent. When youngsters have a difficult time settling down at night, the reassuring presence of a parent helps them to work through the transition from wakefulness to sleep. The physical closeness of a parent is very comforting to many children. Snuggling up to a loving parent creates a safe, protected feeling, prompting youngsters to reveal anxieties that were previously undisclosed.

Sometimes children "act up" in order to get attention from their parents. After long hours away from their working parents, they do not want to let the parents go. Thus they have a hard time saying goodbye at night. If your child begins to act this way, try not to become upset with her or him. Instead, try to schedule a few extra minutes of quiet time with the youngster. This will tell your child you care and may lead to calmer behavior.

Bedtime also affords you the opportunity to listen to your younger children read. Youngsters need encouragement as they tackle the task of learning this complex skill. If you set an unhurried pace at bedtime, even the most reluctant reader might be willing to forge ahead. The children who have already achieved proficiency can show off for an admiring audience or listen to you read alternating paragraphs. Many children adore having parents read to them.

Most children love to talk, especially if they have a captive audience, and, again, bedtime provides the perfect opportunity. David, age eleven, told us, "My dad and I just talk and talk in bed. He tells me how his day went at work and we discuss what happened at school. Sometimes we talk about sports or politics. I like it best when my dad tells me stories about when he was a boy and the kinds of things he did with his brother and parents. We have such a good time together my mom usually has to come in to say it's late and I have to go to sleep."

Older children also need to talk, but the issues facing older youngsters are more complex and require a different kind of adult listening and support. Nighttime conversation gives you the opportunity to discuss a problem your child may be having with a friend or a sibling, in school or at an after-school program. Or it may be the one time when your youngster can admit to a fear of being alone in the house. This quiet time allows you and your child to talk openly about personal matters without fear of interruption.

Playing Games Together

A half-hour or so before I go to bed, I get to choose a game to play with my parents. Sometimes my sister, Marsha, plays too. Monopoly is my favorite. We can never finish Monopoly, so we keep playing for a couple of nights until someone wins. We're pretty competitive but we also have a great time together.
                                            Lauren, age 10

A majority of the elementary school children we interviewed said that they would like to spend some portion of week-night evenings or weekends playing games with their parents. But the number who can boast of having a regularly scheduled time for such activities is low. Again, the reason behind these figures is one we have heard repeatedly from these children: "A lot of times my dad promises to play with me but then he'll say he's too tired or he's not in the mood. I think he just doesn't want to be with me." Children want promises fulfilled. As one ten-year-old said, "I can't count on my mother to play with me even when she says she will." No parents should be insensitive to their child's needs.

Other children are more fortunate. Some younger children told us that after dinner their mother or father plays checkers or cards or board games that can be completed within a short period of time. A few older youngsters remarked that their families have set aside one evening during the week as "game night." As one fourteen-year-old described it, "Thursday is *Scrabble* night in our house. My sister, Jamie, and I finish our homework early. By 8:00 P.M. everyone is usually ready to play. We have some really close games. Those are the most exciting." Other children enjoy this type of closeness by scheduling a time for games on the weekend. For nine-year-old Alan, Saturday mornings are special. "My mom and older brother sleep late on Saturdays, so I have my dad all to myself. We design spaceships with my *Legos* or build models, or play games like *Battleship*. Saturday mornings are my favorite time of the week."

Games allow children and parents to be together, participating in a family-centered activity. Allowing youngsters to choose the game helps them feel that this is their time, and this in turn gives them a sense of control. The games themselves enable children to gain new skills or enhance their present abilities. Thirteen-year-old Donna explained, "Playing chess with my dad taught me to concentrate better. I used to move very fast and lose my pieces right away. Now I take my time because I want to win." Most good board games require some reading comprehension and many expect minimum competence in math. Those that involve strategy planning and execution demand sophistication; others require only luck in the throw of the dice. But all games involve mastering rules, taking turns, the joy of winning, and learning to accept defeat.

Sports and Sporting Events

> *My dad works on Saturdays, so the one day we all have together is Sunday. My parents let us choose where we want to go or what we want to do. My favorite thing is going ice skating.*
>
> Sarah, age 10

Sports play a large role in the lives of many children. Youngsters are energetic and relish a vigorous workout. Their enthusiasm is fostered by fair competition. Don, age thirteen, observed, "My dad is away at least one week each month. But on the weekends when he is around, we play tennis together. My dad plays hard and likes to challenge me to do my best. He's helping me develop my forehand and serve."

A majority of the children we interviewed echoed Don's sentiments, and rated "playing sports" as one of the more popular activities for children and parents to participate in together. Among the sports they most enjoy with their parents are bowling, roller skating, basketball, tennis, swimming, fishing, and hiking.

For most children, sports are another way of playing with parents. You should be especially conscious of your child's level of competence, and guard against turning a friendly game into a combative match. That kind of time together can be destructive to a child's ego. One fourteen-year-old remarked, "My dad is only happy when he beats me. I hate playing anything with him." If you have a strong need to win at any cost, you should choose an opponent other than your child.

All youngsters, regardless of their athletic ability, welcome parental encouragement. As twelve-year-old Elizabeth told us, "My sister Amy is the athlete in our family. She can do anything! My mom decided to take me swimming with her, because I'm always so embarrassed in the summer. We've been going to the pool at the Y twice a week. At first all I could do was three laps and collapse. Now I'm up to ten laps and feel better about myself." Children like Elizabeth may require more parental time and attention than their more agile brothers and sisters. Parents' efforts usually pay off in important ways: increased self-confidence and a greater willingness to overcome obstacles.

You can aid your child's physical development by spending time throwing a ball or teaching him or her how to skate. By choosing an activity your child enjoys, you demonstrate a greater appreciation of your youngster's abilities and encourage her or him to develop skills through pleasurable activity. The most important benefit of your participation in sports with your child is the opportunity to participate with your child in a different way. Unlike most other experiences during the day, sports give you and your child an opportunity to set aside some of the role of parent and child and to simply enjoy the world of play.

At a certain age, your child may join a team sport and your role will change. Children love to have their parents serve as a personal cheering section. Many youngsters say they feel more confident and play better when they know their parents are watching and rooting for them. Their pace may quicken. They may go after the ball a little more aggressively. As one ten-year-old said, "I try harder because my parents are there. Sometimes I try too hard and I mess up."

Your children want you to see them perform and to appreciate the effort they are making. And when your children do not achieve as well as they expected, they need to hear, "You must feel bad," or "Sorry the game didn't go as you wished," or "You had a very strong opponent." Such parental statements of support allow children to express their own dissatisfaction by giving them the opportunity to say, "I could have done better," or "I wish we didn't lose." These statements help children learn to deal with the hurt that inevitably comes from disappointments. Ten-year-old Brian reported, "My mom takes me out for a sundae after every game — win or lose. She tries hard to make me feel better if we get beaten badly. Talking to her helps a lot." Although the youngster begins with the sundae, he ends with his attention on his mother's ability to listen. Remarks such as "You know you should have practiced more," or "I think you could have done better if you had really tried," or "It's only a game, don't be upset," prevent youngsters from voicing their frustrations. Youngsters need to learn to experience constructively both winning and losing, and they need to learn to understand the feelings that come with both results.

Visiting Your Work Place

Sometimes on the weekend if my mom has to go to her office she takes me with her. I usually bring along a book and my drawing pad and pencils so that I have something to do while my mom works. I love sitting at my mom's desk because she has this really neat chair that spins around. She also has a telephone you can speak into without holding it. I like to call my friends or my Grandma Edna and ask them if they can guess where I am. When my mom finishes her work, she takes me out for lunch.

Danielle, age 12

A trip to the place where you work is an adventure for your child. Most children love to be taken on occasional trips to your work place. This allows them to share part of your world and to have a better understanding of the kind of job you perform. In addition, they are able to meet the people you talk about and to develop a mental picture of what you are doing during the day while you are apart from them. Children enjoy sitting at a parent's desk, eating in the cafeteria, and even seeing the bathroom. A fourth grader told us, "My dad works on the thirty-fourth floor. It's really neat going in the elevator, watching the numbers go up and moving so fast."

The children we interviewed enjoy the opportunity to

spend time with a parent. On the ride to and from work they are able to talk with one another without distraction, and the children remember the experience as one that gave them a new view of the parent by seeing him or her at work. Fourteen-year-old Christopher told us, "My dad's a plumber. When he has to make emergency calls on the weekend, he'll take me with him. I help him carry in his equipment and sometimes hand him his tools when he asks for them."

A trip to your place of work can and should be enjoyable if you plan it carefully and wisely. Weekends and evenings are usually the most convenient times for children to visit the work place and most importantly you are likely to be more relaxed at these times. Try to choose a time when having your child along will not interfere with your regular schedule or be disruptive to other employees.

Explain clearly to your child the specific rules of conduct before you even leave the house. One nine-year-old said, "The first time we went to my mom's office she told us we can't run around, make a lot of noise, or disturb other people. She said if we behaved she'd take us out for lunch." Children need to know the *dos and don'ts:* what they will see, what to touch or not touch, and how to greet certain people. They may need to be cautioned not to repeat stories they have heard at dinner, and they should be encouraged to ask you questions about anything that is intriguing or unfamiliar.

You should set a reasonable time limit for the visit, and tell your child your intended schedule. Most children become fidgety if they have to spend too many hours "being good." Your child might bring along a book, homework, a deck of cards, an electronic game, crayons and paper — anything that can help pass the time. You might also pack a snack. Children inevitably become hungry as soon as they arrive at the work place.

No matter how much planning you do, this visit may be difficult and demanding for your child. You should set realistic expectations and try to anticipate your child's responses. Younger children may be more interested in the elevator, water cooler, location of the bathroom, or anyone who gives them a treat. Older children might silently observe the situation without enthusiastic comment. Youngsters of every age will need time to absorb and process the unfamiliar — the height of the building, the rows of desks neatly lined up, the personalities of the various people they meet, and the way their parents interact with others. Children may at first feel awkward because they are being flooded by newness. With each successive visit, they will become more comfortable. Eleven-year-old William told us, "I remember one of the first times I visited my dad at his office. Everything looked so big and strange and I just stayed close to my dad. All these people I didn't know kept coming up to me and saying things like, 'So you're Morris's son. Your dad always talks about you.' It was weird. Now when I go with my dad to work, I know everyone and I have a good time."

Your youngster needs you to be a guide to the world of work. Many children simply do not understand enough about their parents' jobs, and do not even know enough to frame a useful question about their employment. A trip to your place of work will help your child begin to comprehend the larger work world of adults. If you cannot take your youngster to your place of business because you work a long distance from home or you are employed in an industry that discourages visits by family members for safety or other reasons, try to give your child a verbal tour of your work site, being as visual as possible. The purpose of any visit is not only to teach your youngster about your occupation but also to see your place of work through your child's eyes.

Parents Who Travel

> My dad travels about every two weeks. I feel
> like I'm getting ripped off. I just don't see
> him very much.
>
> Jesse, age 9

Many children told us they become angry when their
parents travel extensively. Even when children understand
that their parents must travel as part of their jobs, they
often resent the amount of time their parents are away
from home and from them.

Children are upset when parents miss the events that
are special in their lives. Youngsters want their parents to
be available to attend the school picnic or to watch an important game or to listen to a story of lost friendship.
Youngsters feel especially rejected when parents promise
to come to the school play or piano recital and then fail
to attend. One tenth grader said, "My father was supposed
to be at my dance performance. I kept looking around for
him but he never showed up. He said his plane was late.
Afterward, I just stormed into my room and didn't speak
to anyone. I had practiced my part for a long time and really wanted him to see me."

In addition to becoming angry and resentful, children
become confused when parents' travel schedules are irregu-
lar and the number of days away from home varies from
trip to trip. Children need predictable behavior from the
world around them, and an erratic travel schedule of a
parent can destroy a child's basic feeling that the world
is orderly and reliable. One thirteen-year-old despaired, "I
can never count on my father to be there." This sentiment
is typical of children whose parents frequently travel.

Parents who always resort to gifts to compensate for their
frequent travel do not recover their child's respect. Children recognize when parents are trying to assuage their

own guilt, and many only become angrier. Moreover, parents who try to use gifts to cover for their absence are distorting the meaning of presents. If parents teach children to expect gifts after every business trip, they will find themselves greeted at the door with cries of, "What did you bring me?" instead of hearing, "I'm so glad you're home." Gifts may be appropriate on special occasions, such as after a visit to an unusual area, or if you have been away for a long period of time. But you should be wary of falling into the habit of spending money because you were away on business.

Many children want to know why their parents are frequently going away. Explanations should be geared to the level of understanding of the individual child. Simple statements of fact are best for younger children. For example, a parent might say, "I'm going to New York to buy cloth for my clients. I'll bring home a sample you can use for your doll house." Older children require greater detail.

Your child also needs to know how long you will be away. Marking a calendar to show the dates you will be traveling enables younger children to visualize the length of the trip. You might use a colored pencil to circle the days you will be out of town. Children love to mark off the days as they pass and keep watch over the calendar. For older children, you could write down your schedule and include the names of the places where you expect to stay.

Parents who travel should make a definite effort to stay involved in their children's lives. While you are traveling you should maintain communication between you and your child. Nightly calls home may be expensive and difficult to arrange on a business schedule. However, calling home lets your youngsters know you are thinking of them. Phoning also informs your family that you have arrived safely. Tragedies do occur. Youngsters of parents who travel are often afraid that their parents might be involved in a car accident, plane crash, or hotel fire. They worry about their mother or father who travels and what would happen to them if there was a misfortune.

In addition to telephone calls, children love to receive mail. A note from a parent who is traveling is special. Children delight in reading and rereading postcards from different cities or letters on hotel stationery. Correspondence helps your youngster feel involved in your trip and your business life. Writing and receiving letters is a special form of sharing. Nine-year-old Heidi said, "I sleep with my dad's letters under my pillow. It makes me feel like he's with me."

Children might even be able to accompany a parent on one or two short trips a year. The parent who involves the child in this manner may receive in return a greater measure of respect and tolerance for his or her absences.

Even though you are working, there is time available to relate to your child in a meaningful way. The dilemma of time can be resolved more satisfactorily. *It is up to you to create undistracted time to strengthen and secure your parent-child bond.* Being together will bring a special closeness and vitality to your family.

Chapter 5

You and Your Child's Education

*The education your child re-*ceives will have a significant impact on your child's future success and well-being. Yet the most important factor in a child's success in school is not necessarily a teacher or school or subject. One of the most influential elements in your child's education is *you.* If you take the time to follow your child's progress, set up and enforce reasonable rules for homework, attend regular conferences with your child's teachers, and inform teachers of any crises in your child's life, your youngster will sense that you deeply care about her or his learning.

Helping Your Child to Learn

My mother is an accountant and my father is an architect. They both work really hard. After dinner, they go into their study to do more work. They tell me I shouldn't bother them even if I have a question about homework. They tell me to just ask the teacher when I get to class. What makes their work so much more important than mine?

Mario, age 13

Youngsters want their parents to show an interest in
their work in school. One child in four wished their parents
were more involved in their schoolwork. Many of the children we interviewed were quick to say that parents should
not be too busy or too distracted to pay attention to their
schoolwork. Many children feel slighted when parents fail
to express interest in their assignments or when their efforts in school are not given proper recognition. One sixth
grader complained, "My parents tell me that I am responsible for what I have to do in school. I don't want them
to do my work. I just want them to show more interest
in what I have to do." We found that youngsters reported
feeling increasingly upset when parents' disinterest becomes habitual. One ten-year-old child asked, "Why bother
working hard? My parents don't care how I do anyway."
A high school senior sadly observed, "My parents think
they're the only ones who work hard. They say I've got
it easy. But I have papers and tests and lots of work. I only
wish they cared about all the pressures I feel."

Most youngsters want parents to encourage, direct, or
even push them to sit down and do their homework. Children's schoolwork suffers when they do not receive
parental support. In our written survey we found an
important statistical link: Of those youngsters who said
they had the lowest amount of parent contact, approximately 60 percent saw themselves as performing less well
in school.

Many elementary school teachers told us that a small
but growing number of working parents are failing to provide the guidance and assistance their youngsters need in
order to perform adequately in their studies. These teachers emphasize that both *younger children and older students need their parents to serve as educational boosters.*

The results of our interviews confirm the teachers' concerns. Mothers consistently make themselves available to

discuss school assignments more often than do fathers. Only one third of the students in grades four through twelve said they look to their father when there is a homework question, and slightly over half of these students seek out their mother for advice. Many youngsters added that they would be delighted if their fathers displayed a greater willingness to be involved in their education.

In our research, the results clearly demonstrate that children's academic self-esteem suffers when fathers have little involvement in their children's education. When both parents are interested and involved, children's academic performance is heightened. Many of the children we interviewed spoke in glowing terms about parents who asked thoughtful questions about schoolwork and listened attentively to the answers. This kind of behavior tells your children that you are concerned about the pressures they face even when you have your own work pressures to deal with. Youngsters told us how much they appreciate having a parent express their empathy when they have an especially long or difficult assignment. "If I have to stay up late studying for a test, my dad will usually stay up with me. I'm really glad to have him around," Miriam, an eighth grader, happily revealed. This child tells us exactly what she really wants — moral support and caring.

Your children's confidence is boosted when you praise them and let them know that you think they are capable of achieving their academic goals. Reassuring words help your children meet the specific challenges of the school day and can urge them on to even greater accomplishments. Meghan, a vivacious tenth grader, reported, "My mom and dad always tell me how proud they are of me and the work I do for school. They make me think I can do almost anything."

When you take the time to express confidence in your children's abilities, you create an atmosphere in which

*youngsters are encouraged to value their own achieve-
ments.* Youngsters feel especially good when you compliment them on daily homework efforts. Simple statements
such as "You've really worked hard tonight," or "That
looked like a difficult math assignment you just completed," or "Your history paper shows lots of thought" carry
a powerful message. Your children want to please you and
to fulfill your expectations. If you tell them how proud you
are of their performance, they usually try even harder to
achieve for you as well as for themselves.

Setting Study Rules for Your Child

*My mom used to get angry with me because
sometimes I would forget to do my homework.
Now I have an assignment calendar. She makes
me write down what I have to do for homework each day and when the homework is due.*
David, age 10

Over three quarters of the elementary school children
we interviewed reported that they want their parents
present when they do their homework. These children
recognize that they need parental assistance in some way
— perhaps in helping them organize their homework, or
their time, or encouraging them to begin their work.

Youngsters differ greatly in the amount and kind of help
they need. Some children keep good track of details; others
cannot remember their assignments. Some begin long-term
reports immediately; others procrastinate. Some place their
books and papers in an orderly manner; others can't find
a pen. Some are highly motivated and need little if any
direction; others feel overwhelmed by even the idea of
homework. Some youngsters need help in limiting outside
commitments and in scheduling their time. These children need parental guidance in learning how to schedule

work. Parents provide the motivation many children require. As eleven-year-old Danny bluntly expressed, "When my parents are home, I know I have to do my homework. Besides, it's easier doing your homework when you can ask your parents a question."

Most elementary school children need to begin their work early in the evening. As night advances, younger children become less alert and able to concentrate. Any assignment can begin to appear too long or too difficult. Working parents may also be more patient early in the evening before they succumb to fatigue.

The workload on students grows heavier as they progress from one grade to the next. Junior and senior high school students are assigned papers and readings that require a considerable time commitment. These students must learn to begin their work at a reasonable hour. One tenth grader told us, "I start my work before dinner and spend a couple of hours reading and writing after dinner." Other adolescents may have after-school jobs or other commitments that preclude their beginning homework early, or they may simply need to have a respite from schoolwork before starting their assignments. They need time to unwind, to choose their own activities, to set their own pace. Fourteen-year-old Kevin remarked, "I'm tired of doing work all day long. When I come home from school I just want to listen to music, shoot baskets, or be with my friends. I'm not ready to begin my homework until after dinner."

Youngsters can develop a variety of schedules for doing their homework. Your child should be encouraged to develop one that suits his or her study responsibilities. Children need to feel at least partly in control of their own lives, and deciding when to do homework allows them to feel this way. Further, students who set aside particular hours each night for homework report feeling less pressure and less friction in the home than friends who had more erratic study schedules.

The demands on a child's after-school time will vary according to the child's age, grade, school requirements, and after-school commitments. To help your child develop better homework habits, this list of basic rules for studying at home might prove helpful:

- Allot a specific period of time every day for homework.
- Keep a separate pad or notebook for recording all assignments.
- Mark on a calendar the dates when work is due.
- Choose a work space that is away from distractions and always available at the scheduled time.
- Keep pencils, papers, dictionary, and other school material in a designated place.
- Encourage your child to begin work on time and early enough in the evening to avoid becoming too tired.
- Help your child organize nightly assignments.
- Keep tabs on long-term assignments so that the work is done at a steady pace instead of in a frantic last-minute rush.

Meeting Your Child's Teachers

Our school has conferences at night because so many of the kids' parents work during the day. Sometimes teachers will even come in before school to meet with parents.

Lisa, age 10

School is a significant part of your children's daily lives, and your attendance at regular school meetings shows your children that you are interested in what they are learning and how they are progressing. Through these meetings you gain insight into how your children feel about themselves, their emotional maturity, and their ability to relate to peers.

According to our survey, youngsters want both parents to be involved with their education. Regardless of the age or sex of the child, the working mother is almost twice as likely to attend school conferences as the working father. Eighty-three percent of the children reported in our written questionnaire that their mothers attend parent conferences. Only 43 percent said their fathers attend such meetings. With the growing awareness of the demands facing working parents, many teachers now try to accommodate parents by arranging meetings early in the morning or at other mutually convenient times. In many instances the school tries to make arrangements to suit either mother or father.

The parent-teacher conference is a way to review a child's schoolwork, resolve difficulties, and set new goals. If your child seems to be having problems, you should not wait for a teacher to schedule a conference. Some children told us of attempting to talk to their working parents about an urgent school issue, but neither their father nor mother listen. One fifteen-year-old reported, "My social studies teacher had this group of kids she really liked. I've always gotten an A in this course but she was giving me B's. I told my parents how upset I was at the teacher and my grades. They said they'd take time off from work to go talk to her but they never did. When I received a B as my final grade, my parents finally realized they should have gone in to see the teacher. But it was too late for that."

Conferences are most successful when they are a culmination of close parent-child involvement during preceding weeks. In order for the meeting to benefit you, your child, and the teacher, you should consider it in two parts:

preparing for the conference and the conference itself.

Preparation

Conferences between parents and teachers cannot fully serve their purpose unless the proper issues are addressed. This means you must have advance knowledge about your child's school activities. To clarify the areas you want to discuss, complete the brief checklist given below. Mothers and fathers should probably fill it out separately. Each has a different perspective about how well each child is doing in school. When the forms are completed, compare your answers and then check with your youngsters to fill in any missing information.

CHECKLIST
• Teacher
• Subject or subjects taught
• Child's mark on last report card
• Current homework topics
• What child likes or dislikes about subjects
  — and why

The last item on the list requires your child to confide in you. Your children may be reluctant to discuss certain problems, such as another student who intimidates them or a teacher who seems unduly harsh. It is up to you to make your child feel he or she can speak freely. You may find this difficult if your child criticizes a teacher or another adult, but children's negative comments about a teacher should be taken seriously.

There are times when children feel a teacher does not like them. Sometimes they are right. Not all children and teachers get along well. Conversations with your child should focus on gaining information about the conflict. You should avoid blaming your child with comments like, "There must be a reason why the teacher doesn't like you."

Concentrate instead on a fair and open discussion that conveys information. A complaint such as "She picks on me" is too vague. Parents should ask for specific examples. Your child's statement "Whenever I give the wrong answer Mr. Smith makes fun of me" offers a concrete basis for discussion between you and your child's teacher.

After you have completed the checklist and discussed your child's feelings about school and their teachers, you are now ready to draw up a list of questions to ask your youngster's teacher. Arrange these in order of importance, because you may not be able to cover every topic. If your child is in elementary school, you might be thinking of questions like these:

1. My daughter is shy and says she's afraid to answer in class. Have you noticed this? Does this happen often? What can we do to help her?
2. My son loves to read, but he says he's bored with the books he's using in his reading group. Do you think they could be too easy for him?

If your youngster is in junior or senior high school, you might have these questions:

1. My daughter is very interested in the sciences and is getting top grades. I heard the museum has a course for high school students. Do you think this would be good for her?
2. My son is having difficulty keeping up with the math assignments. Do you think we should be hiring a tutor? Could you give him extra help?

As you prepare for your conference, remember that you and your child's teachers are partners in the endeavor to stimulate your child to think and to learn. You and the teachers share the same goal: the best possible education for each child.

The Conference

The National Education Association suggests that parents and teachers should devote thirty minutes to each conference. You should have the opportunity of meeting with your child's teacher at least twice a year. If your youngster is having difficulty in school, more conferences may be necessary.

Initially, you should be told about your child's specific accomplishments, areas of improvement, and individual talents. You should also ask for and receive a detailed report on your child's academic progress. The results of any standardized tests your child has taken should be carefully explained. You may be given the opportunity to familiarize yourself with the books and other written materials your youngster uses. Finally, you should have access to folders containing samples of your child's work from the beginning of the semester. This will enable you to gain a chronological visual picture of your youngster's struggles and achievements as well as weaknesses.

If necessary, the teacher should spell out what efforts are being made to help your youngster. You should also discuss how you can assist your child. Avenues to explore include summer study programs or tutoring by specialists in the school system, giving math or spelling drills at home, listening to your child read each evening, or making certain that homework assignments are completed satisfactorily.

If your child is gifted, ask how your youngster is being challenged. Your child could be working on a special project, for instance, an individualized computer program. In addition, the teacher may know about an unusual course offered by the local college that might benefit your youngster.

You should also receive a general assessment of your

child's emotional maturity and social development in relation to the class as a whole. After the teacher has given you all this information you could then feel free to ask any of your prepared questions. You should leave the meeting knowing what is expected of your child, how well she or he measures up to these expectations, and how you can help your youngster meet the assigned goals and responsibilities.

To encourage future contacts, teachers might give you a telephone number where they can be reached on certain school days and hours. By filling out the Parent/Teacher Contact Sheet, the teacher is better able to communicate with you as well.

Both teachers and parents have difficult tasks. Teachers must present fair, instructive, and descriptive reports on many children. But they must have conferences with parents in a limited time, and they sometimes feel as if they are the ones being evaluated. Parents need the benefit of the teacher's knowledge and experience, but parents need courage and patience to listen to another adult evaluate their child, sometimes critically. Yet both can achieve their goals with mutual trust and respect.

Sharing Information with Your Child's Teacher

I think my mom is going to lose her job. At least that's what I hear her saying to my grandmother. Listening to them makes me nervous. I've been getting a lot of stomach-aches lately when I go to school.

Suzanne, age 9

Children who are facing a difficult problem in the home may not know how to handle this situation and school at the same time. They frequently mentioned having difficulty concentrating on schoolwork during family crises.

Unfortunately, teachers are often unaware of the upheavals in the home. You help your children by informing teachers of any significant family event that could affect their classroom behavior. The child who cannot sit still, annoys other students, frequently daydreams, is unresponsive to the teacher, is unprepared for class, or demands an excessive amount of attention may be reacting to family stress. Children in crisis feel insecure and not in control of their world. As one sixth-grade child poignantly explained, "Sometimes I feel like I'm sitting at the edge of a cliff. I'm never sure whether or not I'm going to fall off or not, but it sure is scary and my parents just don't hear me." At a critical time like this, your child needs caring, responsive adults who understand the hidden message behind the erratic behavior.

Alert your child's teachers to any notable change in the family routine. By the expression *notable change* we do not mean only the obvious ones like death or divorce. There are changes that seem minor to an adult but can be major to a child. A significant alteration in your employment can affect your child's conduct in school. We met children whose parents were reentering the work force, changing positions, in danger of losing a job, increasing the number of work hours, changing work hours (from morning to night shifts), bringing more work home, and increasing the number of business trips. These children expressed anxiety because their parents weren't around as much or seemed more interested in work problems than in them. Many said their schoolwork was affected. "I just can't concentrate," Sal, a sixth grader, confessed.

Illness, separation, divorce, or death in the family have a substantial impact upon a child's life. Nine-year-old Lily recalled, "My grandfather was very sick this year. He died in December. I used to cry in class because I thought about him so much. My mom came to school to tell my teacher about my grandfather. The teacher was really nice. We even had discussions in class about what makes people sad." Lily was fortunate to have a mother and a teacher who were sensitive to her pain and were able to deal with her in a thoughtful manner.

Try to take time out from your busy schedule to focus on your child's reactions to crises in the family. Then inform the school about what is happening at home. In some cases, you may have to decide on whether or not to disclose confidential information to teachers. Educators recognize the privileged nature of such conversations and should not breach this trust.

When a teacher helps your child through difficult times, acknowledge this effort by expressing your gratitude. Teachers want to provide the best possible educational experience for their students, and positive, thoughtful comments from you and other parents will confirm that they are meeting your children's needs in an admirable way.

Without ever standing in front of a classroom or grading a paper, you play a significant role in your child's education. Your involvement helps motivate your youngster to strive for success in school. A continual interest in your child's daily classroom experiences and homework assignments shows your youngster that her or his education truly matters to you. Careful guidance in setting and following rules for studying helps your child to be better prepared. Attending parent-teacher conferences emphasizes that your youngster's education is worth your time. Your support and guidance are needed throughout their school years.

PARENT/TEACHER CONTACT SHEET

Child's Name _____

Mother's Name _____

Father's Name _____

Mother's Place   Name _____

of Business: Address _____

                 _____

                 Phone No. _____   (Ext.) _____

Father's Place   Name _____

of Business: Address _____

                 _____

                 Phone No. _____   (Ext.) _____

Mother's Best Time to be Contacted at Work _____

Father's Best Time to be Contacted at Work _____

Mother's Home Phone No. _____

Father's Home Phone No. _____

Mother's Best Time to be Contacted at Home _____

Father's Best Time to be Contacted at Home _____

Chapter 6

Before School

The time you spend with your family in the morning sets the tone for the entire day. You need to maintain a proper balance between going to work on time and creating a calm morning for your youngsters. Each one looks forward to a variety of experiences; some pleasant, others challenging, still others boring or uninteresting. How your children face each experience depends in part on how they feel as they leave the house. Do your thoughtful words encourage them to anticipate an exciting, rewarding day, or does your short temper and impatience tell them that their feelings do not matter? It is hard to know precisely the effect our words will have on others, but in the case of children the effect is generally clear. A harsh word from a parent may become a burden that holds a child back from finding pleasure in the school day. But with effort, you shape the early morning hours to create a positive, encouraging atmosphere for your children.

Mornings Together

My house is a zoo in the morning. Everyone is rushing around. My parents are always

screaming that they're going to be late for
work. They bark out orders to us. Make your
bed! Hurry up and eat breakfast! It's a lousy
way to start the day.

Kim, age 11

This comment is typical of the descriptions given by too many children of the early morning hours. Youngsters are upset when their parents speak harshly to them before school; angry words echo in their minds throughout the day.

Too often, hurried parents make their children feel like they are in the way. One eleven-year-old reported, "My mother tells me not to ask her anything or else I'll make her late for work. Why is work always more important than me?" Other youngsters describe parents who react to the pressure of preparing for work by becoming moody. These adults are distant and preoccupied one moment, stormy and demanding the next. Not knowing how to react, children told us that they try to escape the discord by going to their room or leaving early for school.

Most children's schoolwork is adversly affected when parents are consistently unpleasant in the morning. In our questionnaire we found well over half of the youngsters who reported the lowest amount of positive parent contact see themselves as less capable than do their classmates of performing well in school. Many of these youngsters agreed with the statement, "I often feel upset at school." Twelve-year-old Louis summed up his feelings by saying, "It's harder for me to concentrate on my schoolwork or tests if I've just had a fight with my father that morning. When I'm in class, I keep thinking about the mean things he said."

Educators, particularly elementary school teachers, report an increase in the number of children of working parents exhibiting various kinds of troubled behavior. Students may be distracted, sad, angry, fidgety, listless, or withdrawn; many are hungry for their teacher's praise and attention. Children who come to school with such enormous emotional needs pose problems for school personnel. One principal told us, "We have some parents who are so involved in their work and getting to their job that they have little patience for their children in the morning. Some of these children show a lack of interest in work and need a lot more tender loving care than others. These kids really drain our teachers dry." A single harsh word to your child in a morning routine that is otherwise silent and frantic can severely impair a child's ability to learn. Teachers understand that working parents face great pressures in the morning. But teachers' greater sympathy lies with the children who must suffer because of these pressures.

Try to be sensitive to your youngsters' needs in the morning. Is the atmosphere tense? Is your voice razor sharp? Are your parting words an ominous, "Just wait until I get home from work"? Are you sullen and threatening? Once you become more conscious of your unpleasant behavior, you can change the mood of the early morning in your home to one that will benefit your child.

Children thrive on intimate moments shared with parents before school. A hug, a kiss, or a word of encouragement sets a happy tone for the entire day. Getting off to a good start in the morning gives every child greater confidence to face the tasks ahead.

You can create a calmer morning time with your children by rethinking your morning schedule. By rising ten or fifteen minutes earlier a few mornings a week, you can go through your regular schedule at a slower pace, one that allows your children to keep up with you and enjoy your company. Let us go through a typical morning schedule that better accommodates your family.

An affectionate stop at the children's beds to say good morning creates a cozy atmosphere. Children love to have their parents awaken them with a hug or by saying, "I love you." Cindy, a nine-year-old, remarked, "My dad goes to work very early in the morning. My sister and I are still in bed. But he always gives us a hug and kiss and tells us how much he looks forward to seeing us later." These moments help to start a happy day. Many preschool children and younger elementary school children enjoy spending a few warm, snuggly minutes in their parents' bed before the daily rush begins. This is a special time of sharing and feeling close to one another.

Parents who exercise in the morning can easily draw in their children, either to watch and keep them company or to exercise with them. Thirteen-year-old Debbie told us that she keeps her mother company for twenty minutes each morning while her mother rides an exercise bicycle. She added, "Mom says the only thing that keeps her staying on the bike without getting bored is having me around." A sixteen-year-old reported, "My dad and I get up early in the morning and go jogging together. We have some of our best talks on our run."

Finally, by beginning your morning ten or fifteen minutes earlier, you might have time for breakfast with your children. This can be the most important part of your morning routine. Youngsters frequently say that they love having breakfast with their parents. Sitting down allows everyone a few calm moments to share food, conversation, and companionship. You can hear about what is happening in school that day and where your children are going after school. Your children in turn can find out what time you will be home. Giving your children an opportunity to go over your schedule one more time reassures them and helps them cope with any changes in the evening routine that might occur. These few extra minutes together can reinforce a sense of family closeness and create a more positive day for everyone.

Sharing Responsibility

Everyone in my family has a job to do in the
morning. We either have to make breakfast,
clean up, make the beds or walk the dog. We
rotate the jobs so no one gets stuck with
clean up every week.

Sheila, age 14

As children grow older, they are ready to take on greater responsibility for the early morning routine and should
understand clearly what is expected of them. If you believe
children should be dressed before breakfast, you should say
so clearly: "Please be washed and dressed and ready for
breakfast by 7:30 A.M., so we can eat together." Because
of the time constraints, any demands you place on your
youngsters in the morning should be realistic and necessary to do at that moment. Children might have a checklist
by which they are reminded of their schoolwork and other
morning responsibilities. Clarifying who is responsible for
what can relieve some of the pressures on you. Youngsters
may even try to act more responsible and feel more grown-
up because they have their own jobs that contribute to
family harmony.

Children want your praise when they are ready for breakfast on time, set the table, organize their schoolbooks,
make their lunch, or are genuinely cooperative. When you
say, "Thanks for getting dressed so quickly," or "It really
saves me time when you make your own lunch," your children know that their efforts are noticed and appreciated.
One youngster, Lisa, remarked, "I can't make my bed as
well as my mom but I still try and make it every morning.
My mom says she thinks I'm pretty good for nine." Kind
words or a gentle hug from a grateful mother or father can
be a powerful motivator for children.

Mornings Alone

*There's so much to do and so much to re-
member. I'm always afraid I'll forget something. I have to pack my lunch, take my
books, lock the door. A couple of times I shut
the door and forgot my keys. Sometimes I
forget my lunch. I really wish my mom or
dad stayed home until I left for school. I
don't like being by myself.*

                             Mary Ann, age 10

Most elementary school youngsters said they did not like
being home alone each morning and having to get themselves ready for school. For them, this means being responsible for preparing and eating breakfast; organizing their
books, homework, and school equipment; remembering
to take lunch or lunch money; trying not to argue with
siblings; dressing and leaving for school on time; or all of
these things. For many, the list seems endless. Younger
children are often relieved when they get to school because
they are no longer in charge of themselves.

Learning to care for oneself is a slow, uneven process.
Weaning children from adult supervision must be done
gradually, for youngsters become anxious if they are suddenly required to fend for themselves. Many are afraid of
being alone in the morning. Others may even feel they have
been abandoned. The fact is that young children are not
yet ready to handle the emotional and physical demands
of their parents; for a young child these are merely unrea-
sonable burdens.

Before you settle on a particular morning routine, you
should determine carefully how your children feel about
being home alone. To do this, you should ask questions
that will elicit informative responses. "How do you feel
about being by yourself in the morning?" encourages chil-

dren to express their feelings. But a question like "You don't mind being home, do you?" closes conversation. Children know the answer you want to hear, and in most cases will furnish the expected reply.

In general, youngsters are not comfortable without daily adult supervision in the morning until they are in the sixth grade. By this age, children feel more capable of preparing themselves for school. But even these children say they feel more secure when they have a sister or brother to keep them company or are unattended for only a short time.

The consequences of leaving young children alone in the early morning before school are evident to elementary school principals and teachers. An increasing number of students arrive in class improperly fed or clothed. As one principal observed, "No matter how mature any first or second grader may appear, we must remember that we are talking about children who are only six, seven, or eight years old. It frightens me to think of these children home alone in the morning, and they tell me how much it frightens them."

Your young child's feelings are most important. If you cannot be home in the morning, make every effort to provide for supervision of your children before school begins. You may be able to rearrange your work schedules so that on alternate days or weeks one parent stays home until the youngsters leave for school. If neither parent can remain at home, try to find an adult to watch them. An older sibling might be encouraged to take on the responsibility for overseeing the younger children. This may not always work out. They may not be ready, capable, or willing to care for little sisters or brothers.

There may be other older people who are available to watch over your children. A nearby college could have several willing baby sitters. Or you may have a neighbor, friend, or relative who would supervise your child for an hour or so. Ten-year-old Bob reported, "I finally told my parents how scared I was being by myself in the morning. Even though it was only for less than one hour, I didn't like it at all. Now my mom brings me over to my grandmother's on her way to work." Other solutions are possible, and you should consider every alternative before you leave your child alone at home in the morning.

If you must leave your children alone in the morning, help them with their school preparations before you leave for work. Younger children need assistance in selecting clothing that is suitable for the weather. They also require a healthy breakfast. They like being encouraged to organize the books and papers they take to school with them and reminded about after-school activities or appointments. Even adolescents are pleased when parents offer friendly suggestions about what to remember for the school day.

Do not burden children with chores that can be done at other times during the day. Unless a task is a necessary part of the morning routine, it should be deferred until after school. They are less harried and better able to carry out the assignments.

Children love having a parent call home before they leave for school. This final contact until late afternoon or evening can give your child the encouragement that will lead to a happier day. Thirteen-year-old Carolyn told us, "My dad sometimes leaves for work while I'm still asleep. But he usually tries to call from work to say 'good morning.'"

Most youngsters wish their parents would telephone in the morning, but few parents actually do so. More mothers than fathers make the effort, and children would like to see a greater balance. Unfortunately, calling home before children leave for school is sometimes impossible for parents. If you are unable to call your children, particularly those of elementary school age, you might consider asking a relative or friend to be a before-school phone friend.

Cheery messages left by parents can help children feel less alone. Simply writing "I love you" lets your youngsters know you are thinking of them when you are on your way to work. Notes can also be used to communicate information and as welcome reminders. "Your homework is in the living room," "Spaghetti tonight — your favorite," "I'll be home at 6:00," or "You're going to your grandmother's after school — don't forget." As thirteen-year-old Henry pointed out, notes can help children start the day with a smile: "My dad sometimes draws smiling faces and pastes them on the bathroom mirror. That's his way of telling me to have a good day. I save a lot of his pictures and keep them in my drawer."

Arriving Early

Soon after my parents leave for work I go to school. I usually get there pretty early. I have to wait outside until the doors open. Sometimes I get really cold.

Gary, age 10

Some children told us they go to school very early because they are "scared" or "lonely" at home after their parents leave for work. They feel safer at school, where there are people around. In fact, most of the principals we met said they find youngsters already waiting at the front door when they arrive for work. This situation is creating problems for school personnel. One principal of a large school reports, "At least 25 percent of our students come to school one-half hour or more before we open. Some of them are dropped off by parents on their way to work. These parents are uncomfortable with their children being alone. They think we are their babysitting service."

Principals and teachers do not know what to do with children who arrive long before classes begin. Many educators feel that some parents are trying to shift the responsibility for before-school child care onto them. Schools are not prepared to attend to early arrivals. One fourth-grade teacher expressed the frustration of many of her colleagues: "I come early to school to organize my materials for my students. This is my own time. If there are children in the room, they expect me to interact with them. I don't blame them. They are needy for emotional support. But they interfere with my work preparation. We need to work out a better solution than what we have now."

Some school districts are responding to the needs of working parents and their children. They have established programs to supply early morning child care. With before-school drop-in programs, children receive the adult supervision they need until the school day begins. Parents are usually charged a small fee.

One urban school system has opened its doors one hour before the start of the school day to serve breakfast. The warmth of the building is inviting, and the food is healthful and plentiful; here youngsters can enjoy their friends in the early morning in a safe environment. The principal is enthusiastic because he knows that his students are beginning the day with a nutritious diet and sense of well-being. In a suburban school, the administration has initiated an active before-school sports program for children in the fifth and sixth grades. The gym is opened earlier for basketball, gymnastics, and other sports — each activity supervised by teacher volunteers. Attendance is consistently strong, enthusiasm is visible, and the energy level is high. One child reported, "This sure is a lot better than watching cartoons."

The outlines of these programs are simple and can be followed anywhere. If you cannot be with your child in the morning or are unable to provide proper adult supervision, you should investigate before-school programs in your area.

A parent may not want to leave a child home alone. But many may not realize that there are other alternatives. Some may want to believe that their young children "do not mind" being alone. Both assumptions are false. It is in your interest and your child's interest to explore every option. The early morning hours set a tone for your youngster's school day. By reorganizing the first part of your day to include moments to focus on your child, you can better ensure that she or he begins the morning with warm and loving feelings.

Chapter 7

Going to and from School...Safely

*W*hen I listen to the
news, I get scared. I mean some people are
really crazy. Last night, I heard a guy shot his
neighbor. And a lady stole a kid right out of
a shopping cart. It all makes me nervous
about the things that could happen to me just
walking down the street.

Dorah, age 12

Parents do their best to make their homes secure and prepare their children for emergencies that might arise inside their home. But they need to exercise the same awareness of their children's route to school. Many younger children told us that they are anxious about going back and forth to school, because their parents are not available to come to their aid immediately and because they are unsure how to handle the unforeseen. Older youngsters express similar concerns. Leila, a fifteen-year-old remarked, "If some guy tried to grab me on my way home from school, it would take a long time for my parents to even know what happened. They both work pretty far away and I can't always reach them."

Your best response to the problem of sending your children to school is to prepare them to cope with problems that might arise. Young people need fundamental, common-sense rules for self-protection. They need to know how to handle themselves when they go back and forth from school. You may also benefit from talking to your youngsters about your own anxieties concerning their safety. You might want to say, "When you come home from school it makes me feel better if after you lock the door, you call me."

Your children need to know that you are always available to listen to their anxieties or concerns — even when it means calling you at work. Below we describe several techniques for preparing your children to walk or ride safely to school and for making you aware of the safety precautions you can take to help your children.

Walking or Bicycling to School

When I was in the first grade, my father walked with me and my friend, Emmy, to school the first few days. He showed us where the school crossing guards were. He told us never to take the shortcut through the alley.

Arlene, age 10

Walking to school should be a pleasant experience for children, and with a concerted effort you can ensure that your child has a safe route. To increase the margin of safety for younger children, parents should have them walk with an older sibling or with another child. You should first follow the route with your youngsters and familiarize yourself and them with the problems they might encounter going to and from school. Together notice where they have to cross streets and look for street lights and crosswalks.

Be aware of danger spots where youngsters should be especially careful — a busy intersection, railroad tracks, and even dogs that should be avoided. Also, decide on specific places where children could go for help if needed, such as a grocery store, gas station, a friend's house, or the local police and fire station. Once you have settled on a route, you should walk it several times with your children, perhaps before school begins for the year, to give your youngsters a chance to feel more comfortable with the route and to give you an opportunity to know the area in the event of an emergency.

Older children often like to ride their bicycles to school; it's faster than walking and can also be more fun. Many youngsters, however, think of bikes as "big toys" and may not be as careful as they should be. If your child rides a bicycle to school, establish an acceptable route and then review it several times to ensure your child's general safety in the area. Treat the bicycle route with the same attention to detail as the walking route. Look for crosswalks, street lights, and other potential hazards.

In addition to familiarizing yourself and your child with the route, you should also teach your youngster that a bicycle is a vehicle. Your child should know the safety rules for bicycle riders — the traffic laws that apply, what side of the street to ride on, the stop signs to be obeyed, and what they should do if they hear a fire engine or ambulance. Encourage your children to wear bike helmets. The local police and the American Automobile Association present excellent safety programs that can teach your children to be safe and responsible riders.

Taking the Bus or Public Transportation

The big kids sit in the back of the bus so
they can smoke. The little kids don't sit at

*all. They chase each other up and down the
aisles screaming their heads off. The bus is a
zoo.*

Stephen, age 9

Parents are often tempted to assume that once a child
steps onto a bus, he or she is safe for the rest of the school
day. Unfortunately this is not always the case. Children
need to be taught standards of decorum and safety. Parents cannot rely on a bus driver to supervise their children.

If you decide to use the services of a school bus, consider first if your children are mature enough to behave
without constant supervision. Second, you should investigate the quality of the school bus, the availability of seat
belts, the driver's training, and inspection programs.

Many children take a public bus or subway. These youngsters are far more exposed to the dangers of traveling in
the city. Children who use public transportation must be
carefully warned of the dangers and the precautions they
should take. You should take your children on several test
runs before school begins, pointing out the doors to use,
the stops along the way, the bell or buzzer to attract the
conductor's attention, and the route from the station to
the school. Once the school term begins, youngsters should
be encouraged to go with one or more friends. They should
choose a subway car with lots of people and sit as close
as possible to the driver or conductor. If your children use
public transportation, you might keep a small jar of change
in the kitchen or a hallway where your children can find
it easily. Children may also need to be reminded to take
enough money or tokens to return home. An extra coin
or two might be "squirreled" away so they can call you
if necessary.

Encountering Strangers

*I never thought about anything ever happening
to me. But then they found a man dressed up
as a clown waiting for the kids near my
school. He offered some of my friends some
candy and asked them to come into his car.
The ran away so nothing happened but I feel
really scared now. Something could have happened and if it happened once it could happen
again — and it could even happen to me.*

                                        Francine, age 11

Youngsters alone face many dangers, but you can help
to protect them by talking openly with them about ordinary safety precautions. *Your children must be taught
never to talk to or accept rides from someone they don't
know, regardless of what the stranger may tell them.*
Make up stories a stranger might say, for example, that
a parent asked them to pick them up and take them to a
grandparent, or that a mother or father is injured and the
stranger is supposed to drive the child to the hospital. Then
coach your child to say NO. If the school is nearby, your
child should go to the office and report the incident and
determine if any messages have come from a parent. Continue to train your child to say no to any unfamiliar person, no matter how friendly the individual looks or acts.
Your children should understand clearly that they can
never accept favors such as money, candy, or gifts. You
should repeat this lesson as your children grow older to
prevent them from ever considering hitchhiking when they
are late for school or just talking to strangers when they
are older. It is never safe for children of any age to be casual
toward strangers.

Sometimes saying no firmly to a stranger is not enough
to solve the problem. Children should be trained in how

to handle other serious situations as well. Teach your children how to behave when a stranger appears to be following them. The youngsters should avoid a doorway or alley or any other place with no route of escape. If the stranger tries to approach, the children should do what comes naturally: *Scream! Scream!* Police say that "many youngsters feel like a nut but what assailant wants to tangle with a nut?" Youngsters should yell and run away as fast as they can. They should look for help from someone on the street — a neighbor, a pedestrian, a nearby store, a police officer.

Children should take special precautions when they are closer to home or in a residential neighborhood with few or no people on the streets. If they are being followed close to home and no one is in the house, they should *not* enter the house. They do not want to show the person where to find them. Arrange one or two safe places your children can go to in case of emergency. Advise your children that they can go to any house with people they know if the designated neighbors are not at home. Your children should then be instructed to call you and then the police. Help your youngsters to realize that other people in the neighborhood are willing to assist if called upon. Teach your children about your neighbors — who they are and what they do — so that they will feel they know people they can go to for help.

Safety Rules

Children face real danger in the larger world, but with sensible guidance and preparation they can be assured of a greater degree of safety. Below is a list of basic rules that every child should know.

- Allow plenty of time to walk to school.
- Travel with friends by foot, bicycle, or bus.
- Avoid shortcuts through wooded areas or alleys or abandoned places.

- Be alert in traffic.
- Know the location of school crossing guards.
- Cross only at the corner.
- Stay within the crosswalk.
- Never jaywalk or cross against the lights.
- Walk or bicycle in the open.
- Never stop to talk to strangers.
- Know the safe places along your travel route.

Chapter 8

After School

The hours after school can be the best time of day for your child. This is the time when children can most be themselves — play what they want to play and follow their own whims. The afternoon can be more special for your child if together you plan these hours carefully.

Several possibilities for after-school care are available, and you should adopt the one most suited to your child's needs. Each option has its own advantages and all are flexible. As you consider the choices, keep in mind your child's age and maturity and general interests. A child who is painfully shy may learn to be comfortable with other people if he or she can begin with one person — a baby sitter — before joining larger groups. A gregarious youngster may feel deprived if he or she cannot join one or two group activities.

The options described below are designed to meet the diverse needs of children and the difficult schedules faced by parents who work outside the home. Because the choice of child care is an important decision for both parent and child, take your time exploring the alternatives available before you make your decision. Regardless of your choice for after-school care, you may have to make other choices for vacation periods. Several of the options described here can be adjusted for vacation times.

Relatives

> My grandmother takes care of me after
> school. She makes the best cookies, chocolate
> chip with pecans. My mom gets upset,
> though, if I eat too many and can't finish my
> dinner. Sometimes she and Grandma fight
> about it. The other day I heard Mom tell her,
> "I don't want you spoiling her."
>   Beverly, age 8

Relatives such as grandparents, older brothers or sisters, or perhaps even an aunt or uncle may be obvious choices for after-school care for young children. The advantages seem to be obvious: The caregiver is known and trusted. Many parents may feel that their values and wishes will be recognized, understood, and implemented.

Children are usually comfortable with a relative as a baby sitter. Almost half of the children we surveyed had relatives as sitters. Most said they usually felt best with a grandparent. One nine-year-old boy explained, "When Grandpa's here, home really feels like home." Children often find it easier to express their thoughts and feelings with grandparents. Twelve-year-old Nadine said, "Whenever I'm having problems in school, my grandmother is the one I talk to the most."

Grandparents may indeed know the younger parent's values and wishes, but they may not always agree. This can lead to emotional tugs of war between parents and grandparents. One ten-year-old girl overheard her grandmother scolding her father for not making the children dress warmly enough. "They'll catch pneumonia in this

weather if they don't wear hats. It's thirty-two degrees!"
The father responded, "Don't tell me what to do. They're
my kids, not yours." The grandmother retorted, "Well, I'm
still your mother and I will tell you what to do." The child
is left to wonder who is the responsible adult. Repeated
arguments of this nature creates serious conflict in the
child and turns a happy situation into a stressful and unpleasant one.

Before you ask grandparents to act as care givers, try to
reach an agreement with them about rules for the children.
These rules may be revised periodically. You should establish at the outset that the primary responsibility of child-
rearing is yours. Parents and grandparents should talk about
any areas of disagreement in an effort to solve problems.
If you rely on grandparents, remember that they provide
an invaluable service. When they act as sitters, they should
be respected and appreciated by both you and your children.

Relying on older brothers or sisters to act as baby sitters
is often appealing to parents and younger children. We
heard many reasons why younger siblings like to have an
older sister or brother as a sitter after school. A nine-year-
old remarked, "My brother knows what I like and I don't
like." Another told us, "My sister and I are friends. I just
like being with her." Many of the older children are flat-
tered that their parents trust them to act as baby sitters.
Others like the opportunity to learn how to be responsible
for younger children.

But there can be difficulties as well. An older child may
bully a sibling or simply fail to pay attention to the younger
child's needs. Unfair treatment leads to constant bickering
and resentment. Not all adolescents are ready to act responsibly without adult supervision. One ten-year-old said,
"My sister smokes but she said if I ever tell Mom and Dad
she'll kill me."

More than half of the teenagers were dissatisfied with

being the *primary* baby sitter. They complain that younger brothers and sisters refused to obey them. Many have complaints that go far deeper. They resent the fact that their parents expect them to baby-sit day after day. They are angry at having little or no time for themselves and their friends.

Older children are not substitute parents. The baby-sitting job for the younger child should remain occasional. Adolescents are not yet ready to carry the full burden of caring for children. If your teenager agrees to baby-sit from time to time, establish clear rules and responsibilities for everyone. You might say, "Your sister can listen to her stereo for one hour every day after school." Specific rules let everyone know what is expected. A full list of possible rules is included at the end of the next section.

Baby Sitters

> *I've had millions of baby sitters. It seems*
> *that way, anyway. Some were really nice.*
> *They let me do what I wanted. Others were*
> *just too strict.*
>
> > *John, age 10*

At some point every parent must find a baby sitter. It may be for an occasional evening out or every afternoon after school. Your choice of a baby sitter should not be made hastily. Children are great imitators and may be deeply influenced by care givers. Don't be tempted to choose the first sitter who answers your advertisement or the one who lives closest to your home. Unfortunately, some parents spend more time in selecting a new automobile than in choosing the proper care giver for their children. In choosing a care giver or baby sitter, you should consider four steps: collecting a list of possibilities, interviewing promising candidates, supervising the child's first moments with the baby sitter, and evaluation.

In collecting a list of names, begin by talking to friends and neighbors for suggestions. Ask them to spread the word that you are looking for a baby sitter. Investigate the employment office of local colleges and universities; many schools list students who are seeking a position, perhaps in exchange for room and board. Check the telephone directory for a child-care resource center for a list of certified family day care providers. You might also want to post signs in neighborhood stores. Finding a good care giver takes work and patience. It also takes luck.

As you develop a list of candidates, ask your children about their preferences. You may be surprised at the answers. When we asked children that question, their reactions varied. Some boys say they feel "cheated" because they have only female sitters. The gender of the baby sitter should not influence the afternoon activities of children; younger women can be just as adept in athletics as are young men. Others complain of sitters who smoke and "smell up the house."

There are youngsters who prefer sitters of a certain age. Many children say they like teen-agers because they understand them and have the energy to keep up with their endless activity. The complaints children have about teen-agers as baby sitters are the same that parents express about them as adolescents: they monopolize the telephone or eat all the food.

In most instances, adult care givers are the best option. They are more experienced and patient, perhaps from raising children of their own. They are more likely to know what to do in case of an emergency. Parents assume that their children listen to them. But children also complain about some adult sitters who may be too inflexible or not up to the job physically.

Before you begin interviewing candidates, clarify in your

own mind what you are looking for. Do you want someone who will play with smaller children or supervise them? Do you want an adult who will interact with everyone at all times or tend to other work while the youngsters play alone? You should be prepared to state your needs.

When you are ready to interview a number of persons, ask your child to be present. Youngsters appreciate having a role in the selection process and will feel that the choice is partly theirs. The meetings should be convenient for the applicant, children, and *both parents*. Most youngsters said that their father had little or nothing to do with the choice of the care giver.

The interview is a tool by which you gain all the relevant information about the applicant. Ask specific questions as well as broad ones. An effective interview might begin with a general question: "Tell me a little about yourself." If the applicant is a teen-ager, ask about school and the youngster's family. You might also want to ask how the teen-ager would handle certain emergencies. If the applicant is older, you should explore the person's history of work in this area or other relevant employment. Be especially careful to ask older candidates about physical problems that might limit their ability.

You should ask all candidates basic questions on availability, transportation, past experience, and philosophy of child care. These questions require specific, detailed answers. The care giver's philosophy of child care may well determine the length of the relationship between sitter and children. Instead of abstract questions such as "Do you like children?" ask for solutions to concrete problems: "What would you do if Johnny and Wendy were fighting over the use of the telephone?" Try to determine if the sitter's philosophy of child rearing is compatible with yours.

During the interview you should state clearly, preferably in writing, the precise responsibilities of the care giver.

Does the job include laundry, vacuuming, washing, and cooking in addition to child care? You should also state the hours and days the sitter is expected to work, and your feelings about smoking, visitors, and the use of the telephone. Finally, you should state the wages, planned salary increases, extra pay for extra work such as cleaning and mending, vacation days, paid vacations, and other items such as workman's compensation or other insurance.

After each candidate's interview, note your child's reactions to the applicant's answers and statements. Your child could be encouraged to state a preference among the candidates if he or she has one. Consider not only the sitters' verbal responses to your questions but also how they seemed to relate to your children and the children to them. Before making a final decision, ask yourselves: "Does this person seem dependable, mature?" "How do we feel having her in our house with our children while we are away at work?" When you have settled on one person, you should investigate her or his references. These should be current and former clients.

Once the care giver is hired, post the specific guidelines discussed during the interview. This will eliminate the possibility of confusion and arguments over what is expected of everyone. A list of rules is included at the end of this section.

Choosing a baby sitter is not the end of the process. Two more steps are needed. Children often reported that as the new sitter was entering the house for the first time, their parents were ready to go out the door. Be present on the sitter's first day at least for part of the time in order to help your child adjust to the new sitter. Youngsters said they do not feel comfortable with a person they do not know well or at all. Stay while your child shows the sitter around the house, perhaps pointing out special games and play areas.

Finally, after three to five weeks, evaluate your care giver. Know that it takes time for sitters and children to adjust to each other. You should, of course, ask your children about their feelings regarding the sitter. Your children may be vague about their answers. Just as important as their responses is their behavior since the sitter began coming to your home. Are your children comfortable with him or her? Do they usually talk positively about their time together? Or have your children developed behavior patterns — sleeplessness, excessive crying, stomachaches, listlessness, withdrawal, nervous habits, regression to immature behavior, or frequent calling of parents at work? Some parents may prefer to observe the sitter directly by coming home unexpectedly and letting the sitter carry on with the normal routine. You might wish to try this a few times during the first month.

If you are satisfied with the relationship that the baby sitter has established with the children, you should say so. Care giver's efforts should not go unrewarded or unrecognized. If you are not pleased with a particular aspect of the arrangement, this should be clarified. Focus on the specific area of disagreement and attempt to resolve it. If the care giver is sensitive to your child's needs but spends too much time on the telephone, identify this as the problem area and ask the sitter to please monitor the use of the telephone. If you conclude that your care giver is fundamentally opposed to your values, you must end the relationship. You can do this simply by saying, "I'm sorry. It just hasn't worked out."

The process of evaluating your care giver may lead you to review your list of rules and perhaps to revise some. You and the care giver may work out new rules together or your children may raise specific questions. After you have reviewed the list, post a copy in the kitchen or wherever it is accessible. You should also supply a typed and signed statement saying that the care giver is authorized to seek emergency medical care for your child.

Checklist for Care Giver

Care givers should be given a complete set of instructions (listed below) as well as a set of emergency telephone numbers (see the form at the end of chapter 10).

RULES FOR CHILDREN

Television:	hours per day _____
	acceptable shows _____
	_____
	video games per day _____
Phonograph:	hours per day _____
	available records or tapes _____
	_____
Telephone:	number of calls _____
	acceptable times for calls _____
Visitors:	names of friends _____
	_____
	how many per child _____
	length of visit _____
Food:	snacks _____
	meals _____
	allergies _____
Homework:	scheduled times _____
Chores:	list of chores per child _____
	_____
	time for completing chores _____
Pets:	areas open to pets _____
	feeding _____
	cleaning up _____
	_____
	_____

Inside areas   _____
closed   _____
to Play: _____
Outside Play   _____
areas: _____

Visiting Friends: permission needed _____
                    time limit _____
                    distance limit _____

RULES FOR CARE GIVER
Daily   arrival _____
schedule: departure _____
Daily   cleaning _____
activities: cooking _____
                checking homework _____

Visitors for   how many _____
sitter: length of visit _____
Telephone: number of calls _____
                length of calls _____
                taking messages for family
                members _____

                messages to be given to callers __

Medications   _____
for children: prescribing doctor _____
                directions _____

Special   _____
Instructions   _____
for the day: _____
Activities   _____
for child   _____
Activities   _____
for sitter   _____

Parents Alternating as Care Givers

*My mother works Monday through Thursday.
On Friday, she takes care of some of the kids
in the neighborhood. She picks us up from
school. We eat something, then play outside,
or sometimes go to a museum.*

Gerald, age 10

The strong demand for child care has prompted working parents to be especially creative. Some parents have joined others to arrange a schedule enabling each one to take a turn caring for the children of all members. This means that in a group of five parents each might serve as care giver one day a week; in a group of ten, each parent would serve only one day every two weeks.

Many youngsters report that they especially like having their own parent or parents care for them and their friends one day and other mothers and fathers supervise them at another time. The enthusiasm of the children is only one of the advantages. Another obvious benefit is the involvement of parents and their freedom to design their own program. Since parents are exchanging services, there may be little or no cost.

If you want to form a group of parents who will act as care givers, you might want to follow the steps outlined for locating and hiring a care giver. You will need to collect a list of candidates and discuss with them the various points that are covered in the checklist for baby sitters. In addition you should talk about providing and paying for snacks, transporting the children to afternoon lessons or sports programs, and other arrangements. These matters should be settled at the outset to avoid later confusion and misunderstanding. Hold regularly scheduled meetings to talk about general concerns related to child care.

Shared Care Giver

> *We have a woman, Mrs. Johnson, who comes*
> *to sit for a few of us after school. It's nice. I*
> *get to be with my friends. We do a lot of*
> *things together. Once a week Mrs. Johnson*
> *takes us to the library.*
>
> > *Rick, age 8*

A variation on the theme of parents sharing child care responsibilities is several parents sharing the cost of a care giver. Some youngsters reported that their parents hired a baby sitter to watch some children in the neighborhood. Each day after school they go to a different child's house where the regular care giver is waiting for them. The children are able to remain in a home environment after school and enjoy greater freedom of movement. The youngsters might go to Scouts, to dance class, or to religious school, knowing that an adult is waiting for them and available for any emergency. Because the care giver rotates going to different homes every day, no one parent carries the burden of providing play space and snacks. If you intend to hire a shared care giver, follow the steps outlined for selecting a baby sitter.

Group Programs

> *I used to hang around the mall a lot because*
> *I didn't like being home by myself all the*
> *time. I liked it at first, but it got boring.*
> *There was nothing to do, really, just talk and*
> *eat, and look at people. Now I go to a Y*
> *twice a week. I like swimming and basket-*
> *ball and being with my friends.*
>
> > *Andy, age 14*

The number of after-school programs has grown dramatically in response to the number of two-job families. Although more services are needed, parents now have a number of options for organized activity after school, depending on the age of the child and the amount of supervision required. Many elementary school children told us they prefer a structured after-school program to being at home alone. They look forward to playing with their friends and not having to worry about chores or emergencies in the home.

Although adolescents may be considered too old to need constant supervision, youth centers are popular with them because they provide a place where they can feel independent, but have adults around if needed. Teen-agers who are struggling with developing a mature identity appreciate having a place where they do not feel isolated or alienated from those around them.

If you decide to enroll your child in an after-school program, be prepared to investigate several settings to ensure that you find the one best suited to your youngster. You might first obtain a list of facilities licensed by the state, or of programs offered to the public through organizations like the YMCA or YWCA. Identify the facilities that offer the activities you and your child are most interested in.

Be prepared to visit two or three facilities. Request an appointment with one of the persons in charge in order to have someone explain specific policies. Overall, your visit should enable you to answer the following questions:

1. Is the setting suitable to the age of the children?
2. Are the children friendly with each other?
3. What is the range of activities available?
4. What kind of equipment is available?
5. Can children play indoors and outdoors?
6. Do children choose their own activity?

7. Are the children fully occupied?
8. Are the children well behaved?
9. Is the discipline strict, loose, or balanced?
10. How quickly are unhappy children comforted?
11. How are the children's disputes settled?
12. What are the rules for children?
13. How are the staff chosen?
14. What are their credentials?
15. How long has the facility been in operation?
16. What is the teacher turnover rate?
17. What is the child-teacher ratio?
18. What is the general attitude of the staff?
19. Is there an introductory session for parents?
20. How often can parents visit the program?
21. Does the staff provide nutritious snacks?
22. What is the fee and what does it include?
23. Is financial assistance available?

The answers to these questions should enable you to make a reasoned decision that will please both you and your child.

Once you have selected an after-school program for your child, establishing a good working relationship with the care giver is so important. Your behavior shows respect for this person as a professional who is providing a valuable service for your family.

Children told us how terrible they feel when their parents are consistently late in picking them up. They understand that it is disrespectful to the care giver and creates tension. Others view it as a personal slight. As one thirteen-year-old girl said, "Everyone knows what my parents think of me. I mean you don't show up fifteen minutes late every single day if you're excited to see your daughter. It hurts." When you place your child in an after-school program, you are agreeing to abide by rules that are necessary to the smooth running of the program. Follow through on these for the sake of your child's well-being and for everyone else involved.

Try to meet with your child's care giver to talk about how your youngster is doing. This should not be done when you are picking up or dropping off your child. Instead schedule an appointment for a mutually convenient time. Care givers can often spot problems before they become serious and are in turn anxious to know about any special concerns or interests of the parent. You should regard the care giver as your child-rearing partner of the afternoon, and this positive relationship will produce benefits for your child.

Chapter 9

Preparing Your Child to Be Home Alone

*A*t one time or another, most parents who work outside the home confront the dilemma of deciding when their youngster is ready to be left alone at home. Many parents choose to leave their children without adult supervision during the afternoon. This can be a good or bad decision depending on whether or not the child is ready to be at home alone. There is no strict rule by which you can decide if your child is ready. Each child is different and must be evaluated individually. Your youngster's readiness depends on his or her age and maturity, your neighborhood, and the length of time before an adult arrives home. These factors are interrelated and will be considered together. If you determine that your child is ready to spend the afternoon hours at home alone, you should actively prepare your child by developing your neighborhood as a resource, teaching your child how to handle various responsibilities, and making your home safer.

Deciding If Your Child Is Ready

I really feel good that my parents trust me enough to take care of myself after school. I

*know it's a big responsibility but I think I'm
old enough.*   Nancy, age 13

Your child's age is only the barest measure of whether
or not she or he can be left alone. Most younger children
emphatically stated to us that they do not want to be by
themselves after school: "It's scary, and besides, we're
lonely," many said. Some children who are nine or ten years
of age feel they can handle an *occasional* hour alone. By
ages eleven and twelve some are confident that they can
take care of themselves *from time to time* until their
parents return from work. Others are not that secure. In
fact, the majority of junior and senior high school students
recalled to us how anxious they used to feel when they
were home alone. Throughout our interviews, children responded sensibly to the questions of taking on heavy responsibilities too young. *Before they are twelve, youngsters
lack the decision-making skills necessary to function day
by day; primary school children need after-school supervision and young adolescents still need guidance.*

In addition to your child's age, you should also consider
his or her maturity. Youngsters mature emotionally at different rates. They have varying limitations and capabilities.
Some show more common sense than others; some are
more independent, self-sufficient, and self-confident. A
twelve-year-old girl said, "I like coming home and having
a little time to be by myself." But, a thirteen-year-old boy
said he dreaded walking into the house alone. In deciding
if your child is mature enough to be home alone, you must
be scrupulously fair. If your child seems to be truly afraid
of being by himself or herself, you must accept this. Fears
that may seem irrational to you are very real to your
children.

Young people want to share their anxieties with their
parents, and they want their parents to listen to them. You

should ask your children if they want to be alone. If so, for how long? Encourage them to speak openly. Listen to the answers and respect your children's feelings. If your child says she or he does not want to be left alone, honor this request.

If children cannot tell a parent that they do not want to be alone, their unhappiness may soon appear in physical symptoms such as headaches, stomachaches, and nightmares. These are graphic signs of children's terror and stress and could indicate that parents are pushing their children to be independent before they are ready. *Maturity is based upon a child's emotional development, not a working parent's needs.*

If you are ready to conclude that your child is old enough and mature enough to be home alone, you should consider the length of time you propose to leave your child. In our interviews, many children over the age of twelve said they could handle being home alone for limited periods of time. Returning to an empty house every day was overwhelming for younger children. Even adolescents mentioned their loneliness through a long afternoon.

Finally, you must consider your neighborhood — the streets and other houses, or the apartment building and the other tenants on your floor. Some apartment houses offer greater security and protection than others. Some children live in attractive neighborhoods but their home is isolated from other houses. Children need to feel secure in their environment, and you should assess your area from the view of safety for your child.

Using Your Neighborhood

> *My best friend, Cheryl, lives across the street.*
> *I know I can go to her house in the after-*
> *noons. Someone is always there.*
>
> Tisha, age 12

Once you have decided that your youngster can be left alone after school for a certain period of time, you shoudl develop the resources that already exist in your neighborhood — be that a suburban area or an apartment building. Your child should know who is available under what circumstances. For example, most youngsters feel less lonely when they know they can visit friends in the area to listen to music, shoot baskets, play with the computer, or do homework together. Children in an apartment building or in the suburbs should know the neighbor who has an extra key. They should also be aware of at least two neighbors they can call if they are hurt.

By identifying people in your neighborhood who can assist your child when needed, you are helping her or him feel less alone and less isolated. It is difficult for young children to be alone and not feel lonely, but a concerted effort to weave a fabric of neighborhood life for your child can lead to your youngster's greater comfort when home without you.

Staying in Touch by Telephone

> *My dad is a druggist. In fact, the store is just a few blocks from our house. If something happens, I know I can call him and he would be here in a few minutes.*
>
> Leo, age 14

We have already discussed the importance of communicating with your children. When your child is home alone, the telephone becomes a vital link. Youngsters told us how much better they feel when they know they can easily reach their parents. These children have focused on the crucial point: reassurance. If children feel stranded at home, they will not be comfortable being home alone even in their late teens. But children who are told repeatedly that their parents want to talk to them on the telephone and like to hear how they are doing will have far less trouble adjusting to being by themselves. As one thirteen-year-old girl said, "Just knowing that I can call if I have to makes me feel safer." A parent or designated adult should always be available by telephone. And you should reassure your child regularly that you are glad to talk in the afternoon. You want your children to feel that even though they are alone in the house, they are not apart from a larger world.

Preparing Your Child to Be Home Alone

I hate to go home when my parents aren't
there. I always think someone is inside,
waiting for me. As soon as I go in the house,
I check everywhere to see if someone is there.
                                           Donna, age 12

More than three quarters of the youngsters we inter-
viewed said that there are times when they are afraid to
be home alone. Many voiced the fears of children who cannot bear the burden of being alone often: They are afraid of strange telephone calls, strange noises, or strange people coming to the door. Because they feel unprotected at home, the world becomes a threatening, unsafe place.

We were not totally surprised at the overwhelming number of children who are apprehensive about being home alone. However, we were struck by the many children's observations that their parents are frequently unaware of or insensitive to their fears. According to many youngsters, parents either do not listen to their "anxieties" or casually dismiss them as "childish." One ten-year-old said, "When I told my dad I was afraid that some guy in the neighborhood was going to come after me, he told me to stop acting like a baby." This disregard of a young child's feelings is unkind and may even be dangerous.

You should recognize that your child's fears about being home alone are powerful. All children want their parents not only to listen to how they feel but also to teach them how to better respond to dangerous situations that could arise. When your child says he or she is afraid to be alone or hears noises in the house, listen carefully; your child is telling you she or he needs help to feel more safe and secure. By offering strategies on how to cope with possible emergencies, you can considerably lessen your child's anxieties and help your youngster find greater enjoyment in the hours after school.

Preparing a child to be alone does not begin at age eight or ten or twelve. You are in reality laying the groundwork when your child is much younger. You begin when you say to a toddler, "The stove is hot. Don't touch it. You can burn yourself." Later, you might say to a five-year-old youngster, "Don't open the door until you know who it is." At each step, you are teaching your children to exercise caution, to think before they act and to recognize the potential consequences of their behavior.

At first, leave your child alone only for a very short period of time. You might say, "I'm going to the grocery store. I'll be back in ten minutes. While I'm away, make sure the door is locked." You may want to do this occasionally so that your child fully understands the rules and routine. As children grow older and become more self-sufficient, they can spend more time unsupervised. Monitor or review each situation to determine how well your child is doing. Compliment your child whenever she or he handles the new situation well. At a certain point, your child may become uncomfortable and uncooperative. Accept this as a sign that you have reached his or her limit for now. Do not push your child further. Let him or her first get used to this new level of responsibility.

In addition to introducing your child gradually to spending time alone, teach your child the proper responses to various situations. When children know the solutions to problems that might arise, they feel far more confident and relaxed about being on their own. You can teach your child the basic lessons in safety by creating a game called "What would you do if. . ." You should teach your child to give answers to the hypothetical questions beginning with "What would you do if. . ." and ending with phrases like these:

> . . . you were hungry?
> . . . you had a headache?
> . . . you lost your key to the apartment?
> . . . you wanted to visit a friend?

After each question and answer, fill in any missing information. Because children need constant reminders, play this game at regular intervals, gradually incorporating new situations.

As part of preparing your child to be responsible when alone, you should supply simple, basic instructions. Children are comforted and reassured by routines and by knowing they are doing everything they should. Instructions should be clear and concise.

> Please call one of us when you come home after school.
> Let us know if you are going out.
> Take your key and lock the door.
> Come home by five o'clock.

The purpose of these instructions is to guide your child through a period of time when you cannot be there in person.

When your children are older, discuss with them in greater detail the kinds of problems that children alone might encounter. You want your children to learn to be cautious and alert without being too scared to enjoy their afternoon. You also want your children to feel that they are becoming more competent and reliable, not that the world is becoming more dangerous and unreliable. Discuss, for example, what your daughter should do if she is waiting for an elevator alone and a stranger arrives to wait for the elevator. Or discuss with your son what he should do if he thinks someone is following him home. All children should know how to answer the telephone and take a message without giving out any information to someone they do not know.

As you prepare your child to be home alone, spend a few hours envisioning the various incidents of an average day and the kinds of problems that might arise. Think these through and talk about them with your child. Listen carefully to your youngster's concerns. You may be able to answer these questions quickly and easily by listening and giving reassurance, thus preventing them from becoming stressful. For information on resources available to ensure the safety of children and others, see Appendix B, "Community Resources."

Making Your Home Safer

*I'd feel safer if I knew someone couldn't get
into the house.*
                                        Lionel, age 13

Children want their home to be as safe as possible, to prevent their fears about intruders from becoming a reality. Knowing that your home is safe will also ease your mind. The best home security is prevention. For example, the best method of keeping strangers out of the house is to make it difficult for them to get in. The goal of these measures described below is to ensure the security of your child and to relieve you and your child of some of the worry that comes from leaving a child alone at home.

An Alarm System

Most children report feeling safer when their house is equipped with an alarm system. It's like a silent guard watching out for them. They know that the noise is designed to scare away the thief and to alert them, the neighbors, and even the police that someone is trying to break in. Children especially like the panic button next to the door "just in case."

Doors and Windows

Children complain that they are reprimanded because they fail to lock the door. And for good reason. Even when they are at home, doors and windows must be secured. Thirty to fifty percent of home and apartment burglaries occur only because someone failed to lock a door or window. Daytime burglaries are on the increase. You should practice with your child locking and unlocking the doors. You might let your youngster do this occasionally when you leave home together. Also check locks on windows with your child. A window is especially inviting for an intruder. In most instances, the intruder will try to avoid breaking the window and creating a noise that would alert someone to his presence. Therefore, windows should be securely latched.

Different kinds of doors, locks, and windows provide varying degrees of protection. You should consider hiring a bonded professional locksmith to perform a detailed security analysis of your home. Regardless of where you live, your child should always be able to view an outsider without opening the door. In a house, a curtained window near the door allows a child to view anyone who comes to the door. In an apartment building, doors should have a peephole at a level at which the child can see easily. Doors, windows, and locks should never be left broken for any length of time.

Keys

Children like to think of a key as their special protection. While it does offer assurance, there can be no security if the key is under the doormat, in a mailbox, or under a flowerpot. There is no hiding place that is a "secret" from the professional criminal. Each member of the family should have a key. Duplicate keys should be left with a trusted neighbor, a friend, or the building superintendent. Children should know the people who have an extra set.

If your children suspect that their keys have been stolen, they should not return to the house. Rather than risk encountering an intruder, your children should immediately go to the home of a friend or neighbor. There, they should call you and report their suspicions. They should not return until a security check has been made. If the keys are not found, lock cylinders should be changed as soon as possible. Police recommend changing the locks when moving into a new home or an apartment.

Finally, you must instruct your child not to lose keys. If discussions on responsible behavior do not help your child to be more careful with his or her keys, you should consider whether you are asking too much of your child at this stage.

Radios and Answering Machines

When we think of security for the home, most of us think of devices that will physically hinder another person. Yet some of the most effective security devices are simple, everyday gadgets. Leaving the radio on during the day can make a home sound occupied and the familiar noises can be reassuring to youngsters. More than half the children we interviewed said that they like hearing the sounds of a radio when they come home, especially a talk show which creates the impression of conversation. Many youngsters hate to walk into a quiet house or apartment. "It's spooky," one thirteen-year-old said.

You might consider purchasing a telephone-answering machine to screen out telephone calls. If you teach your child how to use an answering machine, your child will be able to interrupt the machine and answer calls from people he or she knows.

Precautions around the Home

Creating a safer house is a complex task that involves careful thought and planning. As you teach your child how to behave responsibly, do not forget to survey the outside of your home for the small improvements you can make to increase your youngster's safety. Below is a list of tips that are designed to thwart or hinder intruders. As you look at your home, you may find other changes you can make.

1. Cut back shrubbery that can conceal a person.
2. Do not leave ladders and tools outside.
3. Do not display your family name on the mailbox.
4. Close the garage doors.
5. Do not leave notes on doors or windows.
6. Do not leave outside lights on during the day.

Preparing your daughter or son to be home alone requires that both you and your child learn to adjust to a new situation. As you encourage your child to take on greater responsibility and to learn about the neighborhood and the protection it offers, you must also find ways of providing physical protection in the home. If you help your child understand the precautions you have taken, your child is less likely to feel abandoned and afraid and more likely to feel both pride and confidence in his or her growing abilities.

Chapter 10

Facing Emergencies

*E*very one of us, at one time or another, will face an emergency. How well we cope may depend upon the preparation we received as children and on the care we have learned to exercise in other difficult situations. As parents, we hope that nothing will ever happen to our children. Yet recognizing the possibility of an accident should compel us to respond to those unforeseen times when they will be alone and face possible danger.

Many of the children we interviewed do not know how to respond to an emergency. They are naturally apprehensive. Accidents of one sort or another are the leading cause of death among children in the United States. Every year, approximately fourteen thousand youngsters lose their lives because of accidents, and an additional twenty-three million children under sixteen years of age are seriously hurt.

Fortunately, most of the accidents that befall children are not severe. But they can still be frightening and require the attention of a medical specialist to ensure that no permanent damage is done. Even a small bump across a corner of a table that turns into an ugly black-and-blue mark can be terrifying to a youngster.

You cannot anticipate or forestall every problem that might occur when your children are at home alone. Scrapes, bruises, and bumps are part of growing up. But good common sense and reasonable precautions can better equip your youngsters to handle emergencies. As your children grow older, you can enroll them in first-aid courses and safety programs. Together you and your children can create a safer and relatively risk-free childhood.

Children also need to learn how to respond to accidents, such as a gas leak, or a threatening storm. They need practical information about first aid, whom and how to call if they are injured, or an escape route from a fire.

Teaching Your Child to Respond to Emergencies

The other day my brother, Gerry, and I were having a wrestling match. All of a sudden, he smashed his head on the side of the door. We were both petrified. He started bleeding like crazy. I gave him a wet towel. Then I called my father. He came right home and took Gerry to the hospital.

Kenny, age 16

Children must be taught to recognize when an emergency that requires an immediate response occurs. An emergency is a crisis of need — usually physical. Your child *must* know that you too will respond if possible. In many instances this means telephoning you for assistance.

Children need to know that help is only a telephone call away. Emergency numbers of a doctor, fire department, hospital emergency room, and neighbors should be posted next to the telephone. A complete list of important telephone numbers, including that of your own home (for children who might forget when confronted with danger), is given at the end of the chapter.

More than half of the children we interviewed thirteen years and under told us that they do not know what to say if they had to call someone other than a parent or neighbor in an emergency. A ten-year-old boy said, "I had to call the hospital and I was shaking. The person asked me all kinds of questions so fast. I blanked. I couldn't even remember my own telephone number." To prevent this from happening teach your child what to say in an emergency. Your child should first identify himself or herself: My parents name is _____. We live at _____. The child should then describe briefly what has happened, not hanging up until the other party has said how to proceed.

The following sections on possible emergencies will give you an outline of situations to discuss with your child. The final section describes precautions you can take to reduce the risk of serious accidents in the home.

Accidents

> *When I was cooking, I spilled boiling water all over my legs. I tried to call my mom and dad, but I couldn't get them. I didn't know whether to call the doctor or not. I hurt so much.*
> *Jennifer, age 15*

Some emergencies require immediate action and professional help. Children should be encouraged to call a physician if they have any injuries or pain. Your child should call the doctor right away if he or she has:

- a cut with profuse or continued bleeding;
- swallowed a poisonous substance such as the wrong medicine, rubbing alcohol, bleach, or a detergent;
- broken a bone or injured a joint;
- injured an eye or ear;
- been burned or scalded;

- begun to choke or finds it hard to breathe, speak, or swallow;
- been bitten by a dog, cat, snake, scorpion, bee, or other dangerous animal or insect; and
- begun to feel lightheaded, dizzy, or that he or she is losing consciousness.

If children are in doubt about whether to call a health professional, they should err on the side of caution.

Gas

> *I turned the stove on, but there wasn't a fire.*
> *I smelled something funny.*
>
> *Carlos, age 13*

An undetected gas leak can cause a major explosion that could swiftly reduce a home to ashes. Tell your children how to respond to a gas leak. If children smell gas, they should open the windows and doors. Teach your older children how to determine if the pilot light is out and how to relight it if necessary. Never use a lighted match or candle to search for the leak. If the gas odor is strong, children should leave the house immediately and breathe fresh air. Finally, instruct your children to go to a neighbor's home and call the gas company. Then they should notify you. If they feel sick or nauseous, they should call a physician.

Storms

> *I was all by myself when it started thundering. I didn't know if it was a hurricane or what. It sounded bad.*
>
> *Nathaniel, age 12*

During our interviews, many children told us that they do not know what to do when it begins to thunder. Teach your children basic rules about storms. If they are older and at home alone, they should be told not to leave the house. Instead, they should turn on the radio for a weather alert. If there is a pet outside, the animal should be brought inside. You should reassure your children that they are safe inside the house. Describe that every home is built with a lightning rod as protection. If you know a major storm is coming, call them and make them aware of the situation. Your reassurance may allay their fears.

As your children grow older, you should explain the differences between electrical, thunder, and wind storms, telling the youngsters what they can expect and how they should protect themselves. In a lightning storm, for example, they should stay away from single trees and flagpoles and towers, and they should never be the tallest object in an open space.

Fire

> When I was little, a fire started in my closet. The fire department said it started because of the wires. Practically everything in my room got burned — my clothes, my books, everything. Now every time I hear a fire engine go by or a smoke detector goes off, I panic.
> *Sandra, age 11*

Only a few children told us during our interviews that they had actually experienced a fire in their home. Yet for these youngsters, terrifying and vivid memories linger for years. They are perhaps lucky to be alive. Home is where nine out of ten people die in fires, a third of them children.

Fire is devious. A smoldering flame can produce fumes — carbon monoxide, smoke, and lack of oxygen — that suffocate both children and adults. If your children see or smell smoke, or hear a smoke detector when they are home alone, they should calmly but immediately go to a neighbor's home and report it. If your children are adolescents, they might look for the cause of the alarm. The problem might be as simple as a piece of bread burning in the toaster, or a pot on the stove in which the water has evaporated. If the youngster cannot find the source *quickly*, he or she should call the fire department and leave the house.

If your children are confronted with a fire they cannot extinguish, they should leave the house or building immediately and rouse other people by shouting as loudly as possible. Youngsters who live in an apartment building should take the stairway, never the elevator. Once they are out of danger, they should call the fire department and the superintendent of the building. They should state their name and address and where they could be located at that time. They should not hang up until the person at the other end of the line understands the circumstances of the emergency. Once they have left, they should be instructed never, *never* to return to the burning house.

You should teach your daughter or son quite explicitly what to do if her or his clothing catches on fire. Children should be told not to run, but rather to lie down and roll back and forth, or they should wrap themselves in a blanket or coat or drapes to smother the fire. If they are outside, they should roll in the dirt, sand, or snow. If possible, they should immediately remove the burning garments, but they should never pull it over their head. They should summon medical help as soon as possible.

Do not wait for a devastating fire to force you into taking precautions. Instead, gather the family together and make a step-by-step plan for an emergency fire escape. An older youngster might enjoy drawing maps of every possible escape route. You might identify two routes: the primary route and an alternative if the primary one is blocked by fire and dense smoke. In an apartment building, show your youngsters the fire exits and designate a meeting place for everyone to meet after they have escaped. Once you have established a plan, practice it regularly. Research indicates that children learn the lessons of fire safety only when they are drilled repeatedly. Authorities therefore recommend that parents take the time to role-play with their children. By practicing these plans, you will help your children to be more secure at home.

Adolescents are more capable of greater responsibility and can be taught standard ways of extinguishing a fire. You should have a fire extinguisher in the home and give clear instructions on how and when to use it. You might also teach them how to smother a cooking fire with baking soda or a top to a cooking pot.

A smoke detector should be purchased for each floor and installed in every living unit near the sleeping areas according to the Federal Housing Administration. Each detector should be tested by you once a month by holding a small candle or lighter six inches below the sensor.

Many fatal residential fires result from carelessness. Matches must be kept out of the reach of younger children. No one should toss a match into a place where it can ignite. When your children are old enough, you might enroll them in a fire prevention course.

Disquieting Telephone Calls

I answered and the person just hung up. It really scared me.
                                    Jeremy, age 11

The telephone can be a blessing and a curse. It brings help in an emergency. It also allows an unwelcome stranger into your home. Children feel frightened when they answer the phone and no one is on the line. The caller may have dialed the wrong number and realizes it when a youngster answers the phone. There could be trouble with the connections. Or a computer may be searching for a line and disconnects when it does not hear a certain tone. These calls are simply part of life and should be ignored.

Children may begin to feel jittery when the phone rings repeatedly and no one answers their hello. If this happens often, it is probably done on purpose. The child should immediately hang up. Other youngsters may make nuisance calls, but no one can be sure who is on the other end of the line. These calls usually occur several days in a row and then stop. You should train your child to say hello once and then calmly hang up. Also encourage your child to phone you when she or he receives such calls.

Many children are confused about how to handle telephone calls that are wrong numbers. Because children are taught to be polite to people, they may think they should give information when it is requested on the phone. *Teach your children that they do not have to and should not give out information over the telephone.* Your child should practice saying, "I'm sorry. You have the wrong number." If the caller engages in conversation, your child should say, "I told you that you had the wrong number," and hang up.

You should take the time to explain to your child the kind of information that will reveal the family's daily routines, schedules, or vacation plans. Names, addresses, and telephone numbers should never be conveyed. Children should be wary of people conducting personal surveys or asking when someone would be home to receive a package. You are teaching your child to control the phone and to deflect the manipulation of adults. Children should understand that if they feel harassed or uncomfortable, they can and should hang up. They do not have to obey a stranger on the telephone.

Seventy percent of the children we spoke with are afraid

of receiving harassing and obscene phone calls. This type of call is disconcerting for both children and adults. But children are especially vulnerable because they are home alone, inexperienced, and easily put off balance and frightened. Prepare your children for this type of call by warning them about its content and then telling them firmly to hang up immediately. Engaging the caller in conversation or expressing fear will just embolden the caller. Although it is not easy, children should try to stay as calm as possible and try not to talk to the caller at all. It is difficult for children to shake the "creepiness" of these calls and you should be willing to listen to your children talk about their feelings if they are upset by such a call.

This type of call is illegal. If your home receives a high number, you should notify the police and the telephone company. The police and telephone company can trace these calls if they seem to be more than random. If your child reports every call to you, you and your youngster can keep a detailed log of time, date, length of call, type of call (obscene, harassing, threatening), sex of caller, voice (high, low, accent, camouflaged), and the person's possible age. Once the party is identified, legal action can be instituted. If your children feel unsafe at any time, they should go to a friend's or a neighbor's house and call you. You must be prepared to interrupt your schedule to listen. For your youngsters, this is a real emergency. When you return home from work, your children may need to repeat the experience again and again in order to work it out of their system. Obscene calls are verbal assaults that invade the minds of youngsters.

Some children told us about a response that seems effective for less serious cases. They keep a whistle near the phone. When they receive an offending call, they blow the whistle into the receiver. This has a devastating effect on the caller's ears. It also has a satisfying effect on the children, for this recourse enables them to act — and act quickly.

Unexpected Callers

I was doing my homework when someone knocked at the door. It was a lady asking to speak to my mom. I think she was selling magazines or something. I really hate it when someone I don't know comes to the door. I feel I should be nice, but what if they're out to do something really bad.

Bert, age 12

Most children told us that they often feel uneasy if the bell rings when they are at home alone. They feel vulnerable and fear that the stranger may threaten them in some way. Your children will be more confident and feel more secure if you teach them certain basic rules for unexpected callers. *Caution* is the password in dealing with strangers. Youngsters control access to the home, and they do not have to let people in. Children are "in charge" when they speak from behind a locked door. When an unexpected caller arrives at the door, children should follow these rules.

- Never admit strangers.
- Open the door only to a known person.
- Do not tell anyone that no adult is at home.
- Do not open the door even a few inches with the chain lock.
- Do not open the door for delivery people. Tell them to leave the package by the door.
- Do not let repairmen into the house.
- Do not open the door for a stranger whose car has broken down or who is in trouble of any sort. Offer to telephone for a garage or the police.

Your child will feel more comfortable turning away strangers if you point out that there are many resources nearby to help people who may come to your door. Your child does not have to respond to unexpected callers and you must emphasize this.

Intruders

> *Just as I turned the key, I thought I heard someone in the house. I was so nervous. I didn't know what to do.*
>
> *Alex, age 14*

One of the most dangerous experiences for any person, child or adult, is facing an intruder in the home. This is a serious emergency and children should be carefully prepared for it. At the very least, preparatory training will help you and your child cope with the anxiety arising from the possibility of an intruder entering your home.

Instruct your children that if on returning from school they notice that something is wrong — an open window or door — they should not enter. Instead, they should leave the area immediately and go to a neighbor's or a friend's house or to the building superintendent. They should call you and the police. They should not return until the home has been checked by responsible adults.

Children may not always notice the signs of an intruder. If they enter and find themselves face to face with an intruder, they should follow three basic rules. One young girl followed these with marvelous results. She walked in and saw burglars at work in her home one afternoon. "I'm sorry," she said. "I must be in the wrong apartment." She left quickly and called the police from a neighbor's apartment. The thief was apprehended because of the youngster's quick thinking and calm approach. The three rules are these:

1. Avoid a confrontation. An intruder may react violently when he is surprised. If he is not provoked, he may not harm anyone.
2. Be passive. Do not try to capture him. Let him leave unchallenged.
3. Get help immediately. As soon as it is safe, telephone the police and give them a description of the intruder: approximate height, weight, clothing, and type and color of the vehicle he was driving.

After an ordeal of this sort, even the most mature child will need a lot of support. Children may no longer feel secure in their own home and will probably require company after school. If you encourage your child to express the deeply felt emotions that result from this sort of encounter, both you and your child will be able to better overcome the experience. Although you may feel uncomfortable talking about such a trauma, both of you need to confront and overcome your fear and anger.

Sexual Abuse

> *I don't like going home by myself. The man next door always comes and talks to me. Sometimes he kisses me and tries to touch me. Maybe he just wants to be friendly but I'm scared of him. I hate it when he gets near me. I would like to tell my mother but she'd probably get mad and say I'm silly.*
> *Michelle, age 13*

One of the greatest fears of preadolescent and adolescent girls we spoke with is that of sexual assault. Since 1976, there has been a 200 percent increase in the reporting of sexual abuse in children. Stories of rape and incest are in the media almost daily. Many children at home alone understandably feel uneasy and vulnerable.

The sexual abuse of children spans all races, economic classes, and ethnic groups. One female in four is assaulted before the age of thirteen, and 10 percent of all reported child assault victims are boys. The sex of the molester is consistent — at least 97 percent are males. The reality may be even more staggering. Experts estimate that only one out of every three or four cases of child abuse is reported. Some authorities attribute 85 percent of all cases of abuse to a relative or friend close to the child and the family.

Children cannot understand why adults want to hurt them in any way. Youngsters who are abused feel helpless and betrayed. When children are sexually assaulted, they face an almost overwhelming constellation of psychological problems — fear, anger, guilt, self-loathing. Some refuse to believe what has happened. They are so ashamed of being violated that they cannot tell anyone about it. Some may even feel responsible for the act, and they fear they will be punished if anyone finds out. Unfortunately, these children become unwitting accomplices in a conspiracy of silence.

Despite the gravity of the problems of sexual abuse and the general confusion among children about sexuality, youngsters told us they find it difficult to talk openly with their parents about these issues. One twelve-year-old girl said, "Whenever it comes up, they just change the subject and ask me to do my homework." Parents will not meet the needs of their children by refusing to discuss this subject; indeed they may even make a bad situation worse. For truth never corrupts. Ignorance only increases a child's vulnerability. A child needs guidance from both parents, and you should avoid the trap of a mother speaking only to a daughter and a father only to a son. If you don't listen to your children's concerns and address these questions, they will receive their information elsewhere, and it probably will not be well-informed.

If your children are old enough to be victimized, they are old enough to be told about both sexuality and sexual abuse. You should tell them the difference between "good" and "bad" touching. *Explain to them that they do not have to allow anyone to touch, hug, or kiss them.* Let your children know that they do not have to accept kisses or hugs from people who make them feel uncomfortable.

Because you are away from your child much of the day, you should be especially aware of your child's verbal and non-verbal clues.

- Does your child become upset when told of a particular person's impending visit?
- Is your child frightened when told that he or she will be alone with a certain baby sitter, relative, or friend?
- Do your child's feelings suddenly change from positive and affectionate to hostile and rebellious when one person's name is mentioned?

You must *listen* if your child says that he or she has been assaulted. Children rarely lie about sexual abuse. This subject should *never* be treated lightly. Gently answer your child's statement by saying, "I'm glad you told me. You were right to tell me." For children worry about telling a parent about an experience that has scared them and need extra comforting at this time. Assure your youngster that the molester will not enter the home again. This may be difficult if the offender is a close relative, but it is necessary. You must avoid punishing the child by allowing the molester to continue to enter the house. Your youngster may require professional counseling. In addition, you should make sure that your youngster is not at home alone.

Sexual abuse is a critical experience for a child. But you can help overcome this trauma by your listening and responding. Children are remarkably resilient, and with care from parents they may be able to better work through even this sort of excruciating experience.

Child Proofing Your Home

My older brother is such a slob. He leaves every-thing lying around — his books, his games, his clothes. Once I tripped over his stuff and sprained my ankle. My mother was so mad at him. So was I. My brother is neater now, not because he wants to, but because he has to.

Carol, age 9

Most accidents occur in the home, usually caused by an object that seems harmless. You may overlook household hazards that you as an adult can easily circumvent, but these may be harmful and even life threatening to your youngsters. The best way to avoid accidents in the home is to prevent them. Walk through your home — room by room — pinpointing potentially hazardous places and devising ways to protect your children from them. Teach about the basic safety rules for each room in the house.

You should begin making your home safe for your son or daughter by removing loose electrical wires and frayed cords. Insert safety plugs in all unused electrical outlets. If you think the circuits might be overloaded, undertake an electrical safety review. If your children are young, install safety latches on cabinets and drawers.

Remove all clutter from floors and stairs. Clutter is the most common cause of accidents in the home. Children move quickly and rarely pay attention to what is on the floor. They easily stumble over scattered clothes, games, and sports equipment.

Scatter rugs can be a hazard. Since they are not secured to the floor, children might easily slip on them and get hurt. Shelves and bookcases should be anchored to the walls and children warned not to climb on them. One fourteen-year-old girl became aware of this danger. "I heard a story about a kid who died because a bunch of cubbies fell on her. When I told my father about that, he nailed our bookcases to the wall." Objects on high closet shelves should be placed so that they cannot fall when a door is opened.

Certain rooms in the home hold more risks for children than others: These are the kitchen and the bathroom. Poisonous cleaning supplies should be kept in a locked cupboard, even if you have older children. Knives and sharp instruments should be kept in difficult-to-reach places. Tools and utensils should be used only with permission or adult supervision. Teach your children how to safely use gas and electrical appliances. Older children should be instructed to remain in the kitchen when the stove is on. Youngsters should not wear loose clothing that could easily catch on fire. Paper and cloth should never be placed on the top of the stove. Pot handles should face the back of the stove so pots cannot be accidentally tipped over. Food spills should be wiped up quickly to prevent children from falling.

The bathroom can be dangerous for several reasons. You should ensure that a tile or linoleum floor does not remain wet and therefore slippery. Children should not be allowed to play here because they can easily hurt themselves on the tubs and sinks. All medicines should be stored separately from household products and never on shelves where youngsters keep their belongings. Each bottle should be clearly marked, and medicines should not be removed from their original containers. You should periodically check for drugs that are no longer used or have passed the expiration date.

Point out the objects in the medicine cabinet and explain the proper usage. Dangerous medications should be kept in a locked cabinet. You should also teach your child how to use a thermometer, peroxide, and iodine; how to dress minor cuts and stop bleeding; and how to apply adhesive tape and bandages. Keep first-aid supplies wrapped in a moisture-proof covering and stored in a cool, dry place.

You should train your children in the use of ipecac syrup or activated charcoal — for accidental poisoning. These medicines should be taken only if directed by a health professional or poison control center. As with all emergencies, speed is essential. If your child thinks he or she may have taken the wrong medicine, the child should find the bottle and call you, a neighbor, a doctor, a hospital emergency room, or a poison control center. Instruct your child to wait for directions from an adult.

The fear of an unforeseen catastrophe can overwhelm children of any age, but this stress can be significantly reduced by facing the challenges squarely and preparing for them as much as possible. By teaching your youngsters common-sense methods of meeting emergencies, you are teaching them not only how to protect themselves but also that they can better control what happens to them. Through this, children learn to balance worry with constructive prevention. This in turn will enable them to meet more of life's less-threatening challenges with greater confidence and ability.

IMPORTANT TELEPHONE NUMBERS

Mother's work number _____

Father's work number _____

Neighbor, friend _____

Neighbor, friend _____

Relative _____

Relative _____

School _____

Police/Emergency _____

Police/Information _____

Fire/Emergency _____

Fire/Information _____

Doctor's office _____

Hospital _____

Ambulance/Local Rescue Service _____

Poison Control Crisis Hotline _____

Dentist _____

Drug Store _____

Telephone Company/Emergency _____

Gas Company _____

Electric Company _____

Apartment Manager _____

Veterinarian _____

Taxi _____

Your Name _____

Address _____

_____

Telephone _____

Chapter 11

When Your Child
Is Sick

*C*hildren, *like everyone else,* sometimes get sick. When children feel ill, they are particularly vulnerable to a parent's thoughtless comments. One fourth grader told us, "When I woke up with mumps my mother said, 'How can you do this to me? I have an important meeting this morning.'" Other children said their parents become angry with them if they wake up sick, as if the youngsters are deliberately trying to sabotage their parents' work schedules or to make life more harried for them.

> *My parents treat my getting sick like a major*
> *crime. They don't even stay home with me*
> *but they try to make me feel guilty for*
> *getting sick. My dad's a lawyer and he talks*
> *to me like he's examining a witness in a*
> *case. He says things like "How come you*
> *were well enough to go out all weekend but*
> *are sick now?" How am I supposed to know!*
> *Walter, age 13*

A child's illness upsets the precarious balance between

work and child rearing. However, with proper planning parents can help meet the crisis. Before your child becomes sick, you should work out a course of action for this emergency, taking into account your child's age and maturity, your ability to take time off from work suddenly, and the availability of alternative child care. You could include two or more approaches depending on the nature and length of the illness. Sometimes your child will have to be at home for one day, sometimes for a week.

Whatever the specific diagnosis, sick children need to be at home, comfortable and comforted. Physicians recommend that children should not be sent to school in the morning if they show any of the following symptoms:

- a fever of 100° (38°C) or higher
- vomiting
- diarrhea
- an undiagnosed rash
- general malaise

If your child has any of these symptoms, keep the child at home. Your child's illness may appear inopportune at best, but it is not intentional. It is a problem, an inconvenience that should be handled with a minimum of fuss. Your primary concern is restoring your child's health, and with careful planning you will be ready for this situation when it arises.

Keeping Your Sick Child at Home

Kids my age are too young to be by themselves when they're sick. I'd be really scared that I wouldn't know what to do if something happened like if I fainted. I'm glad my mom stays home with me. We play games together, like Scrabble. *Sometimes she tries doing work at home but she says it's really*

*hard trying to take care of me and work at
the same time.*
                                    Susan, age 11

Most of the children under twelve said they do not want
to be left alone all day to care for themselves when they
are sick. They are afraid of handling medical emergencies
alone. They wonder what would happen if they become
dizzy, develop a bad headache, start vomiting, or take the
wrong medicine. They become frightened thinking about
what they would do if they couldn't reach their parents
for help. The careful attention of a parent or other adult
can be the best medicine for a sick youngster. As eight-
year-old Bonnie said, "When I don't feel well I really want
my mom or dad to stay home and take care of me. My mom
is usually the one who doesn't go to her office. I feel better having her near me."

There is a striking imbalance in the way parents divide
the responsibility for staying with children who are sick.
An overwhelmingly large percentage of mothers stay home
while fathers infrequently do so. Parents should share this
responsibility, perhaps alternating days for a long illness
or each parent taking part of the day, either morning or
afternoon for one or two days.

In some cases you may not be able to stay home with
your sick child, and you must decide at what age you can
keep a sick child at home alone. Most of the older children we interviewed felt that by the time youngsters are
in the sixth grade, they are ready to take care of themselves
during a minor illness such as a cold or a cough. Serious
ailments would still require adult supervision at this age.
In addition to the seriousness of the illness, consider your
child's emotional maturity, your child's ability to take
medication without supervision, your accessibility by
phone, and the availability of other adults to help in an

emergency. Every child is different, and you should consider these factors carefully even for older children.

If you decide to leave a sick youngster at home alone, reduce to a minimum the length of time your child is unattended. Again, two parents might cover different hours of the day, with one going to work later than usual and the other coming home earlier. You could also try to arrange for a sibling, relative, friend, or neighbor to stay with your child for part of the day, or at least ask a friend to stop by and check on your child.

Regardless of the arrangement you make for visitors for your child, you might place near where your child is resting a telephone and a complete list of emergency telephone numbers (see list at the end of chapter 10). You should also make frequent calls to your son or daughter to offer company and comfort. Being sick can be scary for children and they need to be reassured that this misery won't last forever.

Sending a Sick Child to School

> *Just because my parents didn't want to miss*
> *work they sent me to school with the flu. I*
> *felt horrible and was really angry with them.*
> *My teacher sent me right to the nurse,*
> *because I practically fell asleep in class.*
>   Mary Ellen, age 10

Parents sending sick children to school is a growing and disturbing trend. We are not speaking of children with simple colds, but of children with a fever or a serious rash. A principal in an upper-middle-class suburb said candidly, "Soon after these kids come to school they ask to see the nurse. They tell us that they were sick during the night or that morning." These are children who are sent to school by parents who know clearly the extent of the child's illness. Teachers have no trouble recognizing these children. As one sixth-grade teacher explained, "You can easily tell which children should not be in class. The kids become quiet or else seek extra comforting. They try to perform but just aren't capable of doing schoolwork. They are tired. You know, and they know, they should be home."

Many teachers and principals are working parents who have also faced the dilemma of how to care for sick children. They understand the problems and stress faced by parents, but their primary responsibility is to the students, not to the parents. The school has a duty to protect healthy children from unnecessary exposure to infectious diseases or other ailments. Schools are not infirmaries, and school administrators are therefore obligated to ask a parent to take the child home.

Once the principal has decided that a child should be taken home, the problem is still far from solved. Principals and office staff are finding it increasingly difficult to reach working parents to inform them of their child's illness. Some principals report a more troubling development: parents who refuse to come and pick up their sick children once the school has made contact with them. A principal from a community in which a large number of the parents are professionals commented, "The other morning my secretary tried to call a mother and father at work to tell them that their youngster was ill and needed to be taken home. She finally reached the father. He told her he had a busy schedule that day and to keep his child in the nurse's office until school was over and then to send him home. What kind of reaction is that for a parent to have?"

Schools are not dumping grounds for sick children. Youngsters quite rightly feel abandoned when they discover that neither parent will take them home. They cannot understand why their parents do not care. As one eleven-year-old sadly replied, "When you don't feel well and no one wants to be with you, you can feel awfully lonely and sad inside."

Planning Ahead

If you have a young child, you know that at some time that child will be sick. Since this is inevitable, it is only common sense to plan for this eventuality. You should work out all details of your intended arrangements. Go over them periodically for revisions. If you plan to have good friends drop by occasionally to check on your child, keep these friends aware of your intentions. If you change your schedule at work, go over your arrangements to ensure that they are still suitable.

You should also investigate the options available at work. Some employers have adopted a policy that entitles parents to a specified number of paid personal days to care for sick children. An increasing number of businesses are offering this necessary benefit. Some school systems are particularly receptive to the idea and have already established such a policy for teachers and other school personnel. For instance, the superintendent of a large suburban school district cited a provision of a school contract that allows teachers to stay home with their youngsters in case of illness. The contract specifically states, "Sick leave in addition to personal illness shall include absence because of sickness on the part of a near relative: mother, father, husband, wife, children and members of the immediate household where care of such person is the prime responsibility of the teacher and only until other appropriate arrangements can be made."

This form should be completed by parents and given to each child's teacher or appropriate school personnel.

PARENT EMERGENCY FORM

Mother's Name _____

Business Phone No. _____ Ext. _____

Business Address _____

Father's Name _____

Business Phone No. _____ Ext. _____

Business Address _____

Emergency Contacts

Name _____

Address _____

Phone No. _____

Relation to Child (i.e., friend, aunt, neighbor) _____

Name _____

Address _____

Phone No. _____

Relation to Child (i.e., friend, aunt, neighbor) _____

Name _____

Address _____

Phone No. _____

Relation to Child (i.e., friend, aunt, neighbor) _____

Chapter 12

Family Chores

*M*any *parents believe that* children need to learn to carry out certain chores as part of their role in the family. When children are assigned tasks appropriate to their age, size, and knowledge, they become aware of the skills they will need as adults. They learn to do a job regularly, carefully, and according to instructions. They come to understand that their tasks are part of a larger job, the running of the home, and that they are contributing to the well-being of the larger group, the family.

Nevertheless, we were troubled by the large number of comments from children who find that they are overwhelmed by household responsibilities. An overload of chores causes stress for everyone. It makes children feel old before they are grown. In our survey, almost half the children reported that they have extra chores around the house because their parents work. Many resent being overburdened with responsibilities such as caring for younger siblings, preparing meals, and other general household chores.

If children are assigned too many duties, they can "burn out" even before adolescence. They need free time to grow and enjoy themselves. Youngsters may appear mature and responsible, but they still have their own anxieties of childhood and youth to work through.

Why do I have to work so hard around the house because my parents work? It's not fair. I go to school all day. Then I have tons of stuff around the house when I get home. I don't have a second to myself.

Inez, age 15

Many youngsters are overwhelmed by their parents' demands and insist they are given too much work. A fourteen-year-old girl complained, "Each week my parents give me more things to do. I know, they work. But I feel like I do more housework than they do."

Children will not suddenly become responsible because their parents are working. Teaching children to assume new responsibilities is a slow, gradual, and continuous process. Your expectations must be based upon your child's age, level of physical, emotional, and intellectual development, and distinctive personality traits. Some adolescents are comfortable watching a younger sibling after school, and others are petrified that something might happen. Even if your youngster seems remarkably mature and willing to do chores, you must keep in mind that he or she is still a child. You cannot expect your youngster to work with the same skill or efficiency as an adult.

Usually, beginning at the age of ten, children have their own obligations — homework, music, sports, drama practice, religious school, Scouts, and after-school jobs. In addition, they may be ready to take on chores, but these should not overshadow their interests in other areas. When more and more household chores are assigned, youngsters lose time to be alone or to be with their friends. And thus they fail to learn how to balance work and pleasure. As you begin to assign chores to your child, make sure that your standards are realistic and geared to your youngster's capabilities. In general, your child wants to please you, and reasonable expectations will better allow him or her to do so.

Teaching Your Child about Chores

My parents don't like the way I put away the dishes, but they never told me where things go. What do they expect?

Mel, age 10

When you ask your child to share household responsibilities, take the time to clearly explain the chores to be performed. Children resent being criticized for performing in a certain way when no one gave them specific instructions. Youngsters sincerely appreciate it when parents are specific in their requests. They want you to describe accurately what chores are to be done and the best ways to do them. For example, "Clean up your room" means little to them. Does it mean that there should be no records, dolls, or sports equipment on the floor, or does it mean to pick up "just the clothing"? Your expectations and standards must be continually clarified and reevaluated. You should not assume that your child knows how to run a washing machine simply because it has been in the house for ten years. Skills are acquired gradually, so you should fully and patiently explain the steps in every task.

Children feel better about doing chores and cooperate more readily when they understand the importance of their contribution to the family. To help your children understand their role, include them in the decision-making process. Family meetings are an important way of pooling ideas and distributing chores; when youngsters join in these discussions, there is a greater spirit of family cooperation.

The children we interviewed described different ways of assigning chores. Some mentioned a chores-preference chart. They indicate their feelings about the chore by making a plus (+) next to the task they favor (walking the dog), and a zero (0) next to a job they feel neutral or indifferent about (making beds), and a minus (–) next to a task they dislike in particular (washing floors). Each child is assigned a chore from every category, or each member of the family can draw lots for the household chores. Other children stated that they rotate jobs at intervals to keep from getting bored. A child might set the table one week, clear the table the next week, and dry the dishes the third week.

Several youngsters like the idea of posting the chores on a bulletin board. They can see what is required of them and the changes made in the routine on weekends. Younger children especially enjoy checking off their duties as they complete them.

Sharing the Work Equally

> *I have to do the dishes. I fold the laundry. I help with the cooking. All my brother, Bob, does is take out the garbage on Monday morning.*
>
> *Patricia, age 16*

One of the goals of teaching children about chores is to make them aware that each person has his or her own particular area of responsibility. This includes males as well as females. According to our interviews, next to mothers, adolescent girls are most responsible for household tasks. Not surprisingly, these girls protest that they are required to do most of the work while their brothers get off too easily. Adolescent boys freely admit that they are not expected to do their share of the housework. Many are repeating the pattern of their fathers. As one thirteen-year-old boy stated, "After dinner, my father goes into the den and watches TV. He doesn't even bring his plate into the kitchen."

Of the children surveyed, 78 percent state their mothers do most of the work around the house while only 12 percent mention their fathers as being active and willing participants. Although both parents may work full time, mothers continue to do most of the housework. Male resistance to cleaning and cooking is not limited to any particular age group or economic class. A survey by the American Home Economics Association reports that men married to homemakers spend six minutes per day in the kitchen; men married to employed wives spend just twelve minutes per day in the kitchen. Children are acutely aware of this uneven division of responsibility, and their attitudes tend to reflect those of their parents. As one nine-year-old boy said, "I don't want to set the table, that's girl stuff." But his classmate Rick said, "My dad and I like to go food shopping together. We have a good time."

Assigning tasks according to the sex of children limits their skills and experience and affects their ability to later function as independent adults. Eventually, everyone — male and female — needs to know how to use a stove safely, do the laundry, and perform simple home repairs. Boys can and should wash dishes, scour a sink, vacuum, and cook a meal. A girl can mow a lawn, change a flat tire, and use some power tools. Given the opportunity, boys like to cook and girls enjoy making home repairs.

Children learn adult behavior by example, by imitating those close to them. If parents are responsible about chores, children will more likely be too. This is perhaps a reminder in reverse. As you teach your child the basic tasks of the home, you should remember that your child is studying both your words and your deeds.

Criticizing the Job Undone

*I know I promised to feed our dog and walk
him every day. I love him but I'm not crazy
about taking care of him. I've gotten pretty
lazy about it. My parents have started to say
that it's my job to take care of him, especially since my parents are at work. They
said if I don't take care of him, they're going
to give him to someone who will.*

Joni, age 12

A chore is a job that needs to be done and if it is not
done properly, there are consequences. The main effect is
that a pet has no food or the laundry is not clean. Make
rules clear, the reasons for them, and the results if the
chores are done poorly or not at all. You cannot be vague;
the consequences should be clear and precise. Discipline
should be carried out as soon as possible, consistently, and
fairly, according to the child's age and level of development.

Try to make the tone and content of your verbal criticism as constructive as possible. Success and failure can
become patterns for children. If your children experience
failure too often, they may see themselves as people not
likely to succeed. Children hear from their parents, far too
often, expressions like "You never put things away" or
"You never get it right." This constant harping on failure
can become a self-fulfilling prophecy.

There are constructive, satisfying ways of dealing with
a poor job. One child told us about her family's nag bag.
She and her brothers "redeem" themselves for chores not
done properly through the nag bag. She said, "When we
goof off, we can go to the nag bag to find an additional chore
to do. Our parents don't get so mad at us because they
know we're really trying." This is an excellent way to
teach responsibility and eliminate the unpleasantness of

criticism. Like everyone, children have good days and bad days, and make mistakes. If you maintain your flexibility and a sense of humor your children will learn more willingly and more easily.

Appreciating a Job Done Well

I decided to surprise Mom and Dad by cleaning the house. I washed the kitchen floor. Then I washed the dishes and put them away. Mom and Dad were really happy when they got home. I was very proud.

Sylvia, age 15

Children take pride in a job well done, and they need their parents to acknowledge the results of their efforts. Jed, a junior in high school, reported happily, "I was surprised when I came home late from basketball practice and found a sign on the refrigerator: 'No chores today. Just relax.' " This kind of thoughtfulness reinforces a youngster's sense of well-being. Indeed, youngsters perform better when encouraged by admiration than when continually criticized for their shortcomings.

You could show your gratitude by unexpected occasional gifts and sincere compliments. These thoughtful acts will help reassure your child how much his or her efforts matter to you. As you praise your child, your son or daughter will come to have a deeper appreciation of his or her skills or abilities, and this in turn will enhance your child's self-esteem. By helping with family tasks, your child will feel important and valued, with a deeper understanding of what it means to be part of a family. A son may become aware of the way he walks into the home, being careful not to track in dirt. A daughter may explore repair tasks as a result of her parents' confidence in her abilities. Both children will learn more about themselves.

Regular chores in the home can be either a benefit or a burden to children. By teaching children how to handle small jobs and then gradually increasing the responsibility, parents prepare their youngsters for the day-to-day realities of the adult world. Children are able to learn these tasks, but they are not eager to be overwhelmed with chores. *No parent should be so absorbed in work outside the home that the main burden of the household tasks falls on a youth.*

Chapter 13

Using Time Creatively

O*lder children who are at* home alone in the afternoons have something special: they have time. There are many opportunities for young people who feel comfortable being home alone to use this time to special advantage. Busyness has purpose. Formal education has values. But unstructured hours has a measure of freedom. This can be a time of emotional growth, for richness, and for pleasure. This is a time for thinking, for playing, for sports, for reading, for music, for hobbies, and for television. This is a time to explore.

Although many adolescents say they like time by themselves after school, they also told us they often feel "at loose ends." "Sometimes, I don't know what to do with myself," a youngster will remark. This child has not learned about all the creative activities that can fill the afternoon hours. This child has not discovered the special advantage of free time.

Even though you are working, you can help your children to better cope with being home alone by designing a schedule of activities geared to your child's individual interests, needs, abilities, and your community resources. By teaching your child to use time carefully and well, you will prepare the future adult to build a fuller and richer life.

Television

When I get home from school, I watch the soaps. My favorite is about doctors and nurses. There's this one doctor who's gorgeous. I wouldn't miss the show for anything.

Nancy, age 14

Of the children surveyed, 63 percent say that they are home by themselves for at least a part of the afternoon before their parents arrive home from work. The majority spend their time "glued" to the television set. For television has become the baby sitter for many children after school. A TV set is in nearly every home in America. It is treated as an appliance. Just as the refrigerator is the center of the kitchen, so the television has become the center of the family's recreation.

Television came with many promises. Supporters said it would advance children's language skills, their imagination, their curiosity, their intelligence. And indeed it can. There are excellent programs for children to enhance their emotional and cognitive development. Television can teach a wide range of skills and behavior important to social growth. Television can motivate children to learn and to grow. It can show children the world both as it is and as it might be. There can be moments of profound beauty. More often than not, however, children's television is repetitious and of poor quality.

Unfortunately, studies show that children six to eleven years watch television an average of twenty-five to thirty hours a week. By the time most children finish high school, they have logged 20,500 hours in front of the TV screen and only 16,500 hours in school. Children consume more time by watching television than by eating, reading, and playing combined. In fact, the only activity that occupies more of their time is sleeping.

There is a strong connection between the amount of time spent watching television and academic achievement. The National Institute of Mental Health reported that elementary school children who watch only a moderate amount of television receive higher reading scores than children who are heavy viewers. It is generally conceded that children who watch too much television perform poorly in school.

Parental influence and behavior profoundly affect children's viewing habits. One child typically said, "As soon as my mother and father come home from work, they turn on the TV. So why can't I?" A typical day in a household in the United States can now be divided into almost three equal parts: eight hours of sleep, seven hours of television, and nine hours at work or school, including time for traveling back and forth. Third, fourth, and fifth grade children who watch television the most have parents who are also heavy viewers.

The majority of children told us that they have no restrictions on television usage. They say they usually do not turn off the set until supper or until their parents return from work. Parents who limit their children's television viewing are definitely a minority.

You and your children must therefore take control of the television and not allow it to control you. You should first determine how long each child watches TV. Ask your children to keep a one-week log that records: (1) the name of the program, (2) a brief description of the contents of the show, and (3) the minutes watched. If you hire a baby sitter, ask her or him to help. An eleven-year-old who tried this was shocked by the results: "I couldn't believe it. I actually spent twenty-three hours watching TV that week."

You should be concerned not only with the amount of time your youngsters watch television but also with the contents of the programs. Television guides can help you to choose programs more wisely. Some youngsters told us that during weekends the family sits down together and plans those programs that are acceptable for viewing after school. Other children mentioned to us that from time to time parents call from work and simply ask what programs they are watching.

You should limit the shows your children can watch. Some programs can do real emotional harm to a child, particularly cable shows or soap operas that are saturated with sexuality and violence.

Many television programs contain random physical violence that children should not witness. Studies show that by the age of fourteen, the average child has been exposed to eleven thousand to thirteen thousand acts of violence on television, that is, physical force inflicted on someone else and resulting in injury. During each hour there is an average of 5.7 acts of murder, rape, incest, and other atrocities. Children must understand that violence is not an acceptable mode of behavior.

Other programs contain emotional violence. These are the stereotypes of a race, religion, or sex. Too often, blacks are depicted as subordinates, Italians as criminals, and women as secretaries. Children need your supervision and clarification to challenge these negative portrayals. These are not the images and values of fairness and respect that you want your children to learn.

Television advertisements can also create problems for you and your children. An average child sees more than four hundred commercials a week, more than twenty thousand a year. Eighty-two percent are for foods that are primarily sugarcoated, such as cereals, snacks, candies, and cakes. Twelve percent of advertisements are for toys. This constant pressing of children to want whatever they see can only distort their ability to view and evaluate fairly what is put in front of them.

Consider the effects of television upon your children. For thirty years, the research of social scientists has focused almost exclusively on the effect of the content of a television program. These researchers have largely ignored the less obvious, long-term effects of watching television as a process independent of content. The next time your children are watching TV, look at them instead of the screen. Then ask yourselves, "What are my children doing?" Then ask, "What are they *not* doing.?"

When children are watching television, they are not talking to other people. They are not "doing" with other people. Children are becoming spectators rather than participants. They are living vicariously through other people's lives rather than experiencing life for themselves. Television eclipses real life.

It may be difficult to monitor your child's behavior while you are at work, but you can attempt to draw your child's interest to other activities. When your child says, "I have nothing to do," this is your opportunity to respond more creatively. Now you can explore other possibilities with your children for a more balanced life after school. The following idea is meant to introduce your child to the pleasures of other activities.

Reading

> There is a Wednesday book club for kids at the library. It's pretty neat. The librarian tells us about all the new books that come in. My friend and I take out different books.
>
> *Tony, age 11*

Children who watch television the most usually read the least. How then can you encourage youngsters to abandon the TV set for a good book?

Because reading can be a difficult skill to master, many children are hesitant even about opening a book. Those who find their stride in independent reading may read everything they can lay their hands on. Others may never read anything that is not required and even then unless pressured or coerced by their parents.

You cannot force your children to read but you can set an example when you are home. Some youngsters told us that after dinner when the dishes are put away, the whole family has a quiet time together reading newspapers, magazines, and books. Occasionally they all go to the library. Seventeen-year-old Lori said, "It was natural for me to like to read. My mother and dad always had some kind of book in their hands."

The key is to match the "right" book with the child. Like adults, children read for many reasons — for adventure, entertainment, information, escape from daily routine, fun, laughter. If your youngsters enjoy sports, find books for them on baseball or basketball, football, and sports heroes. There are science books for those intrigued by space travel, chemistry, or the stars and planets. To encourage children with hobbies, there are books on stamp collecting, photography, doll houses, and puppets. Many youngsters enjoy books about animals — dogs, cats, horses.

Even at an early age children want to choose their own reading material. They may not always select what you would like them to choose, but unless their preferences are inappropriate for their age and maturity, you could allow them to follow their own inclination. The value of reading skills and the importance of developing reading as a habit far outweigh the reservations you might have about their choice of reading material.

You should not pressure your children to read books that don't interest them, unless, of course, they are required as homework. Your only result will be to destroy their desire to read. Children should also not be expected to read books that are too difficult for them. When a youngster says, "I don't like to read," that may mean, "I don't understand what I am reading." Books should reflect not only the child's age but also his or her reading level.

Many children love building up a home library of books that are their "very own." Having their own bookcase or book shelf instills in them a sense of pride. They are able to tell at a glance what books they have already read and what they may look forward to in the future. Other youngsters are interested in magazines such as *Humpty Dumpty, Jack and Jill, Cricket, Science World, Sports Illustrated,* and *Cobblestone.*

Introduce your child to the public library as early as possible. Very young children can find picture books and become comfortable in an environment of books and readers. Librarians provide valuable guidance in the selection of materials according to an older child's interests, needs, and level of comprehension. Borrowing books from a public or school library is a privilege to which every child is entitled.

Finally, you and your children can read to each other a few moments or an hour in the evening. This is a family activity that children told us they treasure.

Music

> As soon as I come home, I turn on my stereo
> as loud as I want. I like to be alone. No one
> tells me to turn it down.
>
> Keith, age 13

Many children told us that one of their greatest joys is

being home by themselves after school or with their friends, playing the music they like without adults nagging them. For people of all ages, there is power in music — to soothe, to comfort, to inspire, to excite, and simply to give pleasure. Music is a natural part of children's lives. They enjoy having their own radios and tape recorders so they may enjoy their own musical tastes. Music is music whether it's Beethoven or the Beatles or Tina Turner.

Your children's tastes may not coincide with yours. There are generational differences. Your musical needs are different from your children's, and certainly youngsters have the right to make their own choices. You can only insist that the volume is kept at a reasonable level and encourage variety in your children's musical tastes.

The musical atmosphere at home — or lack of it — can play a significant role. Some youngsters told us how impressed they are when they attend as a family a musical, ballet, or children's program by a symphony orchestra. They like to discover the wide range of music from *Peter and the Wolf* to Gilbert and Sullivan to contemporary music to classical and opera. Even youngsters who listen only to their own brand of music are often attracted by other strong melodies and decided rhythms such as Sousa marches and Strauss waltzes. And many children enjoy listening to the compositions of Chopin, Mozart, and Offenbach. Music — all kinds of music — can be a companion to children when they come home from school.

Instruments

> When I come home from school, I have to practice the piano. It sometimes gets boring but I kind of like it. I'm getting pretty good at it.
>
> *Sharon, age 12*

Many children derive genuine pleasure and satisfaction from learning to play a musical instrument. If you think your child has talent or interest, you could expose her or him to several instruments to ensure that the appropriate one is chosen. Before you purchase an expensive instrument, arrange for your child to test the instrument in school and possibly consult the school music teacher. Instruments can first be rented. If you hire a private instructor, select a teacher who will blend in with your child's needs, personality, and schedule. If lessons are given in your absence, careful scrutiny must be given to the instructor's moral calibre in addition to his or her musical knowledge and method.

The purpose of learning to play an instrument is to enjoy another area of life than can bring both understanding and pleasure. If a teacher is too critical, the children may begin to feel overly critical of themselves. Your child should not feel forced into constant practice. Some children complained that they were forced to play an instrument at too early an age. "My parents started me on the piano when I was in the first grade. I know that I never asked to play it," a thirteen-year-old girl said. She was plunged into a routine of lessons and practice. Both she and her parents were ultimately filled with regret. She said she can still hear her father saying, "With all the money I'm spending, you didn't even practice today!" She finally finished with the teacher and the piano in the third grade. Any other kind of musical instrument was summarily dismissed throughout her childhood.

Your standards should be realistic. Youngsters may enthusiastically practice when they are first learning to play the instrument, but later they may rebel if they feel they are being pushed too hard. Children are not always willing and conscientious in their musical training. From time to time, this is to be expected. You want them to enjoy themselves and learn about music. You should not be training them for the concert stage.

Art

I have lots of art supplies — markers, colored pencils, pastels, paints. Sometimes when I'm by myself, I draw or paint. It all depends on my mood.

Rose, age 14

Art can be a wonderful experience for children. Life cannot only be expressed in sounds but in shapes and colors and textures. A child's interest begins with scrawls and scribbles. Soon they enjoy painting with their own fingers, using tools like paintbrushes, and shaping figures in clay. Artistic excitement usually continues as they grow older.

Art is used by children at home alone as a way to express their feelings visually. They are able to utilize their own imagination, originality, and symbolic understanding in various creations of paint, graphics, calligraphy, clay, and collages. They can behold their own handiwork. Art is not a specialized activity for talented children. A youngster's work should be accepted for what it is — a wonderful opportunity for self-expression.

You can help maintain your children's interest in art by providing decent materials, a place to work, and a central place to display the finished product. Youngsters enjoy seeing their artwork on a refrigerator door or a bulletin board. A suitable storage place enables children to be organized and to have direct access to their immediate materials at all times.

Hobbies

My friends and I collect baseball cards. A few afternoons a week, Jonas and Tyler come

to my house and we trade. The other day,
I traded a Willie Mays for a Ted Williams. I
have a Lou Gehrig, and a Warren Spahn. I
really want a Babe Ruth.
                                    Buzzy, age 11

Children rarely embark on a hobby in earnest until they are seven or eight years old. Even then, their focus is likely to shift many times. Hobbies reflect children's interests, and they could change as they grow in knowledge and skills. Hobbies should be chosen by the youngster, not by a parent.

Some children enjoy collecting — from stickers to stamps to coins to sports cards to recordings to insects. They arrange the items in order to distinguish one from another. They may then attempt to complete a set or fill in the gaps in a series. Collecting teaches a child organization and patience. Children also learn cooperation by sharing information and trading items with others. Many youngsters especially enjoy this aspect of collecting. Other hobbies may teach different skills. Handicrafts — from pottery to model building — can improve coordination and dexterity.

Children can turn to a hobby for as long as they want whenever they want. Their investigations can be a welcome break in the day's routine and a creative way to relax after school.

Games

Chess is exciting. My grandfather taught me
how to play. I play with Melissa, the girl
down the street. We talk about a lot of
things. Sometimes she wins and sometimes I
do. That's okay. We're both pretty good now.
                                    Carolyn, age 12

There are many kinds of games that children can play after school, from card games, checkers, chess, backgammon, to board games like *Trivial Pursuit, Risk,* and *Boggle.* Aside from the fun of playing them, games can be excellent educators. They can challenge children to think, teach fair play, and improve coordination and attentiveness.

Jigsaw puzzles train the eye to isolate shapes, colors, and patterns, and train the child to develop patience. *Scrabble* and crossword puzzles build vocabulary. Some computer games teach marketable skills, but others have the same flaws as television. Some video games' themes are concerned with violence, shooting, and conquering. There are aggressive games that involve blowing up planets and waging a nuclear war. One particular game scores points by running over video people as they scramble for safety. Like television, video games can encourage passive play. You should try to be aware of what programs your youngsters are using, and discourage the use of games which promote antisocial behavior.

Cooking

I started cooking when my mom went back to work, because when I got home, no one was there to make me anything to eat. So I began to experiment and came up with some really wild concoctions. Some were pretty horrible. But after a while, I got to know what things went well together. Now I do a lot of cooking. I like doing it when I get home from school.

                          Harvey, age 17

Children are hungry when they come home from school and will eat whatever appeals to them. For this reason it is important that they learn about nutrition. They should know that orange juice is better than a soda, and fresh fruits, cheese, and raisins are more healthful than potato chips.

Youngsters enjoy learning how to prepare simple snacks. Recipes should suit the child's age. After the snacking, cooking, and eating, your children should be taught how to clean up. This may mean you will have to instruct them carefully and demonstrate by example. Small children especially need to be shown clearly what is expected of them.

Sports

> *After school, my friend Cory and I go to the playground and play some basketball. He's really good. He can get jump shots like you wouldn't believe. I'm a better blocker. We really work up a sweat.*
>
> *Roberto, age 11*

Many children who enjoy sports like to be involved in a team sport after school. "I feel really close to everyone on the team. We work hard together and it feels so great when we win," said one teen-age girl. As her comment indicates, children learn important social skills such as cooperation and teamwork as well as athletic prowess. Many communities sponsor well-supervised sports programs for children of all ages.

Children differ from each other, mentally and physically. Where some might be quiet, introspective, and prone to sedentary activities, others always seem to be in perpetual motion, never staying in one place long enough to cast a shadow. Not all children will demonstrate the same ability in athletics or the same interest in team sports. These youngsters may seek other physical activities more compatible with their personalities and abilities such as bicycling, table tennis, jogging, and swimming. Not all youngsters need to play tennis. Walking alone or with friends is still considered one of the best ways to exercise.

Pets

> *When I open the door and see my dog, I'm not afraid anymore.*
>
> *Carlos, age 13*

Some children told us that their parents purchased pets for them when they first began coming home alone after school. One twelve-year-old boy said, "My mom and dad didn't like my being in the house all by myself so they bought me this beautiful collie, Kelev." A dog in the house or in the yard can be good protection against an intruder. But an animal provides far more than protection.

Children love pets. Youngsters seem to have a natural feeling for these active and somewhat helpless creatures. Pets can make children feel strong in a world of powerful adults, and give them a feeling of being forever loved. Animals also afford children an opportunity to develop responsibility and express kindness. Pets need to be fed, walked, and cared for. In return, the animal offers warm, unconditional attachment.

Children may complain that they don't like being responsible for their animal. They may ask, "Why do I have to do the feeding, the walking, the cleaning up?" Yet almost all the youngsters we interviewed told us how happy they are to have a pet to keep them company after school. Children may complain, but we should not underestimate the depth of their attachment and the importance of the pets in their lives.

The list of activities for children to occupy their time at home after school is limited only by the imagination. Your youngsters need your thoughts, suggestions, and experience. Most children do not have the understanding or maturity to plan a satisfying afternoon, day after day. They need your help to structure their time, to make choices that will contribute in some way to their well-being, physical and intellectual development, and fun and relaxation. After school, your children need time to unwind and to enjoy life. You can help them to spend their time in a way that will make their hours richer, more fulfilling, and more creative.

The Children Speak

Six hundred forty-one children from across the country wrote a story about how it would feel to be at home alone each day. The students were given the beginning sentences and asked to complete the story.

> *P.L. is a young person about my age who lives with a family where P.L.'s mother and father both work Monday through Friday. P.L. is a very thoughtful young person, and after school P.L. goes home, knowing that Mother and Father won't be there until later. P.L. starts to think...*

The most pervasive feelings presented by the children was that of loneliness, a sense of isolation, of being apart from their parents. Many were scared and afraid of noises and possible intruders. There were fantasies that something dreadful would occur to their parents while at work. Some believed that their mothers and fathers had left the home as a rejection of them.

On the other hand, some children wrote about a wonderful sense of freedom in being home by themselves. They enjoyed the quiet and solitude. They liked the feeling of independence. Yet they couldn't help wondering, "How would life be if my parents weren't away, working?"

Let us listen to the children speak their own words and express their own feelings.

169

Loneliness

She wishes that her mother and father were home, or she had some brothers or sisters, or even friends that she could play with. Then she starts feeling sad and lonely. When her mother and father come home, she talks to them about one of them staying home and how she's starting to feel lonely and scared all alone.   *age 11*

Maybe her parents could take out more time to be with her. Her parents should have a friend or neighbor with her so she won't feel so lonely. Or they should even try to change job times to get home earlier in the day if possible.   *age 13*

I'm always alone because my parents are always working. I have no sisters or brothers to hang around with. I don't like it. It really bothers me. One thing I can do about it is talk to my parents about it and tell them how I feel.   *age 15*

He thinks about his parents and others he loves. The house is very quiet and quite gloomy, so he is sad. He becomes very lonely. He goes into his bedroom and begins to read on his bed when he falls asleep. He awakens to his cheery thoughtful parents who embrace him. He is now happy and cheerful.   *age 15*

Finding Something to Do

He better start finding things to do with himself after school so that the time flies by more quickly.   *age 12*

What can he do while his parents are gone? He goes upstairs to clean his room. His mother will be very happy to see he cleaned his room without being told. After he finishes his room, he goes to the living room and watches TV while he does his homework. After he finishes his homework, he calls his friend and they go to play basketball and he leaves a note on the kitchen table.   *age 14*

Why don't I take a friend home with me? We could listen to some tapes or records and just talk. We can tell jokes, have something to eat or drink. We could make plans to see a movie or go to

a concert or just go out and hang around together.   *age 15*
What can I do? Things that my parents wouldn't especially
enjoy when they're home. Put an album on and work in the
living room. Maybe have some friends over.   *age 17*

Fear

What will happen if I hear strange noises in the house and then
I see something move???? *age 9*

He thinks about strange things around his house. Burglars, mur-
derers, and rapists. Finally his parents get him a sitter and his
anxieties are reversed. *age 12*

What if a stranger comes to the door and I don't know what to
do? I hope that the neighbors are there so that I could go over
there for a while and stay till my parents get home. *age 13*

If his parents will ever get home. He becomes so scared and
frightened that he hides beneath the covers. The phone rings.
He jumps. He looks around the room, knowing something is
going to happen. *age 15*

Independence and Freedom

She thinks that she will be fine. If anything happens, she can
handle herself. But if she can't, she knows who to call. She is
very sure of herself when she goes home, but feels it will be more
pleasant when her parents get home. *age 11*

He is growing up. He is now independent and can handle being
on his own. He begins to look forward to this time when he can
be by himself, he begins to value his time alone. He feels he
has responsibility being on his own. *age 17*

He is important and has his own privacy to do what he wants.
He can learn a sense of responsibility. He also has his parents'
phone numbers in case of an emergency and he can also take
very good care of himself. He has a chance to invite friends over
and they watch TV and become more mature together. *age 17*

Now I can do anything I want. I think I'll call my friend and

stay on the phone for hours. This is great!   *age 15*
I feel freedom! I can walk in the house without having to be told
to do something. I feel like a weight has been lifted.   *age 17*

How nice it's going to be to have the house to herself. She loves
her mother but it's nice to be alone at times just to think. She
can have a cigarette and no one will know.   *age 17*

Rejection

They don't love me anymore. They're always working.   *age 9*

He feels left out in the world. He often plays with his dog when
he comes home from school. He also plays by himself up in his
room. That's the only thing else for him to do. He has lots of
friends but doesn't often play with them, because he worries
about his parents.   *age 12*

My parents are never home and they don't care about me. Why
can't one of them stay home? It's not fair to me at all.   *age 13*

His family (mother and father) don't care. He starts doing bad
in school and developing delinquent after-school habits.   *age 14*

That his parents don't want to be with him and that's why they
are not home when he gets home from school. If they wanted
to spend time with him, they wouldn't always be working and
they would make time for him.   *age 17*

Parents Are Working to Give Children a Good Life

How much I love them. But I wish they didn't work so hard.
I know they love me and that's why they work, so they can do
fun things with me. I sort of enjoy being here because I look
forward to them coming home and loving me.   *age 11*

It's O.K. if they have to work. I know they still love me and they
are working for me. If they didn't work, we couldn't eat or drink.
Sometimes I worry about them working all the time. But I
always find something to ease my mind. When they come home,

I feel happy because now I have someone to talk to.   *age 13*

His parents are trying to make his life better and he is learning to be independent. Which are two important "pluses" in his favor.   *age 16*

Her parents are working so they can get money to give her good shelter, food, and clothing. She enjoys being alone to think. She knows her parents are working to support the family.   *age 16*

Something Will Happen to Their Parents While They Are at Work

What if my mother doesn't come home? Maybe the building burned down or a speeding car knocked her over.   *age 9*

He thinks something happened to his parents because it is late and they are not at home. He panics and feels very scared. He cries for about an hour.   *age 11*

Maybe his parents won't come home after work. His imagination starts to run wild and starts thinking where he will go and what he will do.   *age 15*

Wanting to Help Their Parents

My parents work too hard. I'm going to have a party for them with a big cake. They're going to love it. I'll invite all their friends and relatives. It will be fun!   *age 9*

Maybe I should think of a way to surprise my parents when they get home. Let's see, I think I'll clean up the house and work on the laundry. Then, maybe I'll cook something for supper. Boy, they'll be surprised. They think that my sister is the only one that ever does anything around here. You wait until they see what I can do!   *age 13*

How he could help out his parents when he gets home. He thinks of ways to budget his time between his studies and responsibilities so that when his parents get home he could have the time to be with them and talk. He is aware of things around him and the responsibilities of taking care of the house and how

to discipline himself when temptation to go off with his friends
arises.   *age 18*

Ambivalence about Both Parents Working

I wonder if children that don't have both parents working are
luckier than I am. I'm home by myself. It's very lonely. I hope
nothing happens to me or my parents.   *age 10*

Maybe when I'm older, I'll be just like my parents (I think it
best that I stay with my kids). I kind of don't like being alone.
I'll make sure I don't do this with my kid(s).   *age 10*

I wonder what it would be like to have both parents home. To
be able to talk to them when I want to, not have to wait until
they come home. I go out and play and forget about home for
a short while but it always comes back that both of my parents
aren't home. I sometimes eat alone because they are late. But
when they're home I feel happier and more secure.   *age 13*

Am I unlucky that both parents work, or should I be happy that
they work? They are bringing home money to support me, and
anyway I need time for myself. I am kind of glad I have this time
to do my homework, watch television. I don't mind at all.
                                                        age 17

Do my parents really love me? They're never home. She thinks
why am I always alone? She talks to her parents about how she
feels and she begins to realize that they both work so that their
family will be able to live comfortably. She now knows her
parents really love her and care for her. She is relieved and
happy!!   *age 18*

Community Resources

The Community Working Together

Children should be taught to respect and trust the police. Youngsters need to understand that police are there to help them. Law enforcement officers want children and adults to call them whenever suspicious persons or actions are observed — a stranger entering a neighbor's house when the neighbor isn't home, or unusual noises like a scream or breaking glass. Many people hesitate to call the police for fear of being a "nosy neighbor" or a "crank." Still others assume that someone else has already called. Even if these suspicious situations have innocent explanations, the police department would rather investigate an uncertainty than be called in after the event.

In recent years, many communities have organized safe homes and block parents in cooperation with the police. Volunteers are screened by local police to provide emergency service or shelter to children who may be threatened by an adult, a bully, or an animal. In many towns, children recognize the homes by the sign *Block Parents* or *Neighborhood Watch* prominently displayed in the window.

Below is a list of a few of the local organizations around the country that support children until their parents return from work. This list has been compiled by the School Age Child Care Project of the Wellesley College Center for Research on Women, Wellesley, Massachusetts 02181. We are grateful for their research.

CITIZENS' CRIME WATCH SAFE HOMES PROGRAM
Citizens' Crime Watch, 5220 Biscayne Boulevard, Suite 200, Miami, Florida 33137. Citizens' Crime Watch is a nonprofit organization devoted to fighting crime. Its Safe Homes Program for elementary school children is primarily geared to those children who live within a two-mile radius of a school and who walk or ride a bike rather than take a bus. The prime benefits of Safe Homes are that they discourage crime; give more security to students and parents; alert students to dangerous situations outside home and school; teach students to identify and describe persons and vehicles involved in crime; unite the schools, parents, police, and neighbors; offer a vital community service; contribute to public awareness on crime prevention; and offer children a safe haven in case of an emergency.

DETROIT COALITION FOR A UNIFIED BLOCK PARENT PROGRAM
Michigan State PTA, 1011 North Washington, Lansing, Michigan 48906. Under the leadership of the Detroit PTA Council, the Detroit Public Schools, the Archdiocese of Detroit, and the City-Wide School Community Relations Council joined together to form the Detroit Coalition for a Unified Block Parent Program. The coalition established the following goals: (1) to ensure the health, welfare, and safety of the public, private, and parochial school students as they travel to and from school; (2) to involve the local school-parent group; (3) to secure the cooperation and involvement of the entire community, including the police, private citizens, places of worship, and members of the business and professional communities; (4) to inform parents and students about the dangers and how to avoid them; and (5) to establish an official window sign used by all program participants.

EMERGENCY BLOCK PARENT PROGRAM:
THE BIG RED "E" PROGRAM
Fowler PTA, 6509 West Roosevelt, Phoenix, Arizona 85043. This program is designed for children from ages five to eighteen who need a place to go in case of an emergency. "E" parents participate as often as seven days a week (when they're not home, they must remove the "E" sign from their window). Approval from the

school superintendent, principal, and local police is necessary before a Big Red "E" program can begin in a school district. All volunteers participate in emergency procedure training, which includes handling stress, basic first aid, and when to call the police.

SHAWNEE MISSION AREA COUNCIL OF PTA:
BLOCK MOTHER PROGRAM
Shawnee Mission Area Council of PTA, 7235 Antioch, Shawnee Mission, Kansas 66204. Their handbook lists six steps that a PTA should take before beginning a block mother program: (1) assess the need; (2) obtain support from the school district and superintendent; (3) work with the city council or local public safety committee; (4) confer with the police department and ask assistance; request a police review and training session for all block mothers; (5) consult with legal counsel and consider liability for the PTA and block mother; and (6) check insurance coverage.

Telephone Services

For children without adult supervision after school, a telephone help line can provide youngsters with needed emotional and practical help. Volunteers listen to youngsters' feelings of loneliness and fear and give advice to the children on what to do about minor accidents, such as wet clothing, books left at school, or a sick pet. The hot lines make referrals if the situation warrants it.

CONTACT-SYRACUSE
CONTACT-Syracuse, 958 Salt Springs Road, Syracuse, New York 13224. The program is twenty-four-hour telephone counseling service staffed by trained volunteers. The service is strictly confidential and anonymous. Volunteers never ask for names nor give out their own last names (many use pseudonyms). Volunteers who receive fifty hours of training regularly make referrals to other community social service agencies. The service has expanded to include a specially designed hot line for children at home alone after school.

PHONEFRIEND

American Association of University Women, State College Branch, P.O. Box 735, State College, Pennsylvania 16801. An after-school telephone help line for children, "PhoneFriend" is sponsored and operated by the State College Branch of the American Association of University Women in cooperation with the State College Women's Resource Center. Volunteers staff telephones at the Resource Center from 3:00 to 6:00 P.M., Monday through Friday. "PhoneFriend" does not replace usual emergency referrals but acts as a backup to existing emergency services.

Coping Skills

There are new, exciting programs that teach youngsters of many ages safety skills, emergency procedures, and general self-reliance. Consult the Red Cross in your area.

BASIC AID TRAINING

American Red Cross, Minneapolis Area Chapter, Youth Services, 11 Dell Place at Groveland, Minneapolis, Minnesota 55403. This is a six-session course designed to train and certify community leaders (teachers, nurses, and scout, church, and recreation leaders) in a basic safety and first-aid class. The curriculum includes what to do in case of fire, bleeding, poisoning, choking, animal bites, and water safety. The class is designed for fourth, fifth, and sixth graders. High school youngsters are trained, certified, and given academic credit for teaching the class to local elementary school children.

COOPERATIVE EXTENSION SERVICE

901 Wythe Street, Alexandria, Virginia 22314. The service is a six-session survival course for children, ages eight to thirteen, with an emphasis on "coping skills." The curriculum includes how to get along with your siblings, what to do when your friends drop in for a visit after school, house rules, coping with fears and loneliness, and safety and emergency procedures. Each session ends with a cooking lesson to acquaint children with nutrition, kitchen safety, and equipment.

GROWING UP SMART
Council for Greater Boston Camp Fire, 38 Chauncy Street, Boston, Massachusetts 02111. The program is an adaptation of the "I Can Do It" program of the Buffalo-Erie Council of Camp Fire. "Growing Up Smart" is described as "an activity program to help young people explore common sense decision-making and self-reliance skills for the home." The course includes five sessions, which are designed for both younger children who are learning home survival skills for the first time and older children who are preparing for the responsibility of baby-sitting.

THE HOMEMAKING ELEMENTARY LEARNING PROCEDURES PROJECT (HELP)
Cranston Public Schools, 845 Park Avenue, Cranston, Rhode Island 02910. HELP is a domestic survival course for children in grades three through six. The project is integrated into the regular school curriculum. Children learn to use sewing machines, needles, cooking and cleaning appliances, and carpentry tools.

I'M IN CHARGE: A SELF-CARE COURSE FOR PARENTS AND CHILDREN
Kansas Committee for Prevention of Child Abuse, 212 West Sixth Street, Suite 301, Topeka, Kansas 66603. "I'm in Charge" is a self-care education course for upper elementary school children and their parents. The course's philosophy stresses that "each latchkey setting is the joint responsibility of parent and child." The course consists of five sessions — one for parents, three for children, and one for parents and children together. The sessions cover personal safety skills, emergency procedures, and care of younger siblings. Of special note are the sessions that help parents and children communicate and negotiate rules and self-care procedures.

ON MY OWN
Michigan Pine and Dunes Girl Scout Council, 1533 Peck Street, Muskegon, Michigan 49441. "On My Own" is an educational program designed to teach elementary school children to safely and successfully cope with being at home alone until their parents

return from work. The course meets twice a week for four weeks and is open to both boys and girls, Girl Scout members and non-members. Topics include snack preparation, games to play alone, fire prevention, telephone manners, using the library, and basic first aid.

P.A.L.S. (PROGRAM TO ASSIST LATCHKEY STUDENTS)
Bridgeview Elementary School, 780 South Thomas Avenue, Bridgeview, Illinois 60455. The P.A.L.S. program is designed to be used with students in kindergarten through sixth grade and to be included as part of the regular elementary school curriculum. The program is taught primarily by the teachers. The curriculum includes first aid, comparison of life styles, baby-sitting, safety, nutrition and health, and being on your own at home.

PREPARED FOR TODAY
National Office, Boy Scouts of America, 1325 Walnut Hill Lane, Irivng, Texas 75062. The program is designed to help children ages six to twelve cope with being at home alone. It is meant to facilitate communication between parents and children. Four themes emerge: "taking care of yourself when you are alone; helping your family deal with problems; stopping what might be an emergency; helping to care for younger brothers and sisters." Six different kinds of skills are taught in the manual, including preparing snacks, knowing your neighborhood, home safety rules, self-esteem builders, and problem solvers.

Bibliography

Parenting

Biller, Henry, and Meredith, Dennis. *Father Power*. Garden City, N.Y.: Anchor Press/Doubleday, 1975.

Brazelton, T. Berry. *On Becoming a Family*. New York: Delacorte, 1981.

———. *To Listen To A Child: Understanding the Normal Problems of Growing Up*. Reading, Mass.: Addison-Wesley, 1984.

Bernard, Jessie. *The Future of Motherhood*. New York: Penguin, 1975.

Boston Women's Health Collective. *Ourselves and Our Children*. New York: Random House, 1978.

Callahan, Sidney Cornelia. *Parenting: Principles and Politics of Parenthood*. New York: Penguin, 1974.

Carmichael, Carrie. *Non-Sexist Childraising*. Boston: Beacon Press, 1977.

Chess, Stella, and Whitbread, Jane. *Daughters*. New York: New American Library, 1978.

Chess, Stella; Thomas, Alexander; and Birch, Herbert G. *Your Child Is a Person*. New York: Penguin, 1965.

Comer, James P., and Pouissant, Alvin F. *Black Child Care*. New York: Pocket Books, 1975.

Elkind, David. *The Hurried Child*. Reading, Mass.: Addison-Wesley, 1981.

Erikson, Erik. *Childhood and Society*, 2nd ed. New York: Norton, 1963.

Faber, Adele, and Mazlish, Elaine. *How To Talk So Kids Will Listen & Listen So Kids Will Talk*. New York: Avon, 1980.

Fraiberg, Selma. *Every Child's Birthright*. New York: Basic Books, 1977.

———. *The Magic Years*. New York: Scribner, 1959.

Galinsky, Ellen. *Between Generations: The Six Stages Of Parenthood.*
New York: Times Books, 1981.

Gerzon, Mark. *A Childhood for Every Child: The Politics of Parenthood.*
New York: Outerbridge & Lazard, 1973.

Ginott, Haim G. *Between Parent and Child.* New York: Avon Books,
1975.

Gordon, Thomas. *P.E.T.* New York: New American Library, 1970.

Kanter, Rosabeth Moss. *Work and Family in the United States: A
Critical Review and Agenda for Research and Policy.* New York:
Russell Sage Foundation, 1977.

Kohl, Herbert. *Growing With Your Children.* Boston: Little, Brown,
1978.

Lawrence, Margaret. *Young Inner City Families: Development of Ego
Strength Under Stress.* New York: Behavioral Books, 1979.

Lerman, Saf. *Positive Parenting for the Eighties.* Minneapolis: Winston
Press, 1980.

LeShan, Eda J. *How to Survive Parenthood.* New York: Random House,
1965.

———. *Natural Parenthood: Raising Your Child Without a Script.* New
York: Signet, 1970.

Levine, James A. *Who Will Raise the Children? New Options for
Fathers (and Mothers).* New York: Bantam, 1977.

Lewis, Robert A., and Pleck, Joseph H. *Men's Role in the Family.* Minneapolis: National Council On Family Relations, 1979.

Long, Lynette and Thomas. *The Handbook for Latchkey Children and
Their Parents.* New York: Arbor House, 1983.

McAdoo, Harriet Pipes. *Black Families.* Beverly Hills, Calif.: Sage Publi-
cations, 1981.

Miller, Jean Baker. *Toward a New Psychology of Women.* Boston:
Beacon Press, 1976.

McBride, Angela. *The Growth and Development of Mothers.* New York:
Harper & Row, 1973.

Pogrebin, Letty Cottin. *Growing Up Free: Raising Your Child in the
Eighties.* New York: McGraw-Hill, 1980.

Packard, Vance. *Our Endangered Children.* Boston: Little, Brown, 1983.

Rivers, Caryl; Barnett, Rosalind; and Baruch, Grace. *How Women Grow,
Learn, & Thrive.* New York: Ballantine, 1979.

Rogers, Fred, and Head, Barry. *Mister Rogers Talks with Parents.* New
York: Berkley Books, 1983.

Spock, Benjamin. *Baby and Child Care,* rev. ed. New York: Pocket
Books, 1977.

————. *Raising Children in Difficult Times.* New York: Norton, 1974.
Stinett, Nick; Chesser, Barbara; and DeFrain, John, eds. *Building Family Strengths.* Lincoln, Nebr.: University of Nebraska Press, 1979.
Winn, Marie. *Children Without Childhood.* New York: Pantheon, 1981.

Adolescence

Bell, Ruth. *Changing Bodies, Changing Lives.* New York: Random House, 1980.
Blos, Peter. *On Adolescence.* New York: The Free Press, 1962.
Elkind, David. *All Grown Up & No Place to Go.* Reading, Mass.: Addison-Wesley, 1984.
Erikson, Erik. *Identity Youth and Crisis.* New York: Norton, 1963.
Ginott, Haim G. *Between Parent and Teenager.* New York: Macmillan, 1969.
Kagan, Jerome, and Coles, Robert. *Twelve to Sixteen: Early Adolescence.* New York: Norton, 1973.

Psychology

Ackerman, Paul, and Kappelman, Murray M. *Signals: What Your Child Is Really Telling You.* New York: Dial, 1977.
Axline, Virginia M. *Play Therapy.* New York: Ballantine, 1969.
Fassler, Joan. *Helping Children Cope — Mastering Stress Through Books and Stories.* New York: The Free Press, 1978.
Miller, Mary Susan. *Childstress!* Garden City, N.Y.: Doubleday, 1982.
Missildine, W. Hugh. *Your Inner Child of the Past.* New York: Pocket Books, 1963.
Napier, Augustus Y., and Whittaker, Carl A. *The Family Crucible.* New York: Bantam, 1978.
Satir, Virginia. *Peoplemaking.* Palo Alto, Calif.: Science and Behavior Books, 1972.

Schooling

Bailard, Virginia, and Strang, Ruth. *Parent-Teacher Conferences.* New York: McGraw-Hill, 1964.
Chess, Stella, with Whitbread, Jane. *How to Help Your Child Get the Most Out of School.* Garden City, N.Y.: Doubleday, 1974.
Gordon, Ira, and Breivogel, William. *Building Effective Home-School Relationships.* Boston: Allyn and Bacon, 1976.

Kappelman, Murray M., and Ackerman, Paul. *Between Parent and School*. New York: Dial, 1977.
Miller, Susan Mary, and Baker, Samm Sinclair. *Straight Talk to Parents: How You Can Help Your Child Get the Best Out of School*. New York: Stein & Day, 1976.

Self-Esteem

Axline, Virginia. *Dibs: In Search of Self*. Boston: Houghton Mifflin, 1964.
Briggs, Dorothy Corkille. *Your Child's Self-Esteem*. Garden City, N.Y.: Doubleday, 1970.
Coopersmith, Stanley. *Antecedents of Self-Esteem*. San Francisco: W. H. Freeman, 1967.
Rogers, Carl. *On Becoming a Person*. Boston: Houghton Mifflin, 1961.

Television

Kaye, Evelyn. *The ACT Guide to Children's Television*. Boston: Beacon Press, 1979.
Moody, Kate. *Growing up on Television: The TV Effect: A Report to the Parents*. New York: Times Books, 1980.
Williams, Fredrick; LaRose, Robert, and Frost, Frederica. *Children, Television and Sex-Role Stereotyping*. New York: Praeger, 1981.
Winn, Marie. *The Plug-In Drug: Television, Children and the Family*. New York: Viking Press, 1977.

Organizations and Other Resources

Action for Children's Television, 46 Austin Street, Newtonville, Mass. 02160
Association for Children and Adults with Learning Disabilities, 4156 Liberty Road, Pittsburgh, Penn. 15234
Day Care and Child Development Council of America, Suite 507, 711 14th Street, Washington, D.C., 20005
Education Development Center, 55 Chapel Street, Newton, Mass. 02160
Family Service Association of America, 44 East 23rd Street, New York, N.Y. 10010
Fatherhood Project, Bank Street College of Education, 610 West 112th Street, New York, N.Y. 10025
Federation for Children with Special Needs, 120 Boylston Street, Boston, Mass. 02114

Foster Grandparents Program, Letchworth Village Development Center, Box 53, Theills, N.Y. 10984

National Association for Retarded Citizens, 2709 Avenue E East, P.O. Box 6109, Arlington, Texas 76001

National Association for Women, 425 13th Street, N.W., Suite 1001, Washington, D.C. 20004

National Foundation for Gifted and Creative Children, 395 Diamond Hill Road, Warwick, R.I. 02886

Index

Academic achievement, amount of time spent watching television and, 156

Academic self-esteem, 22, 24–25, 28, 65

Accidents: in the home, 135–137; as leading cause of death among children, 121; teaching child about responding to, 123–124

Activities, *see* Creative activities

Adolescence, importance of building high self-esteem in, 26–27

Advertisements, television, 157–158

Affection, expressions of, 28–32

Alarm system, equipping house with, 118

Alone, preparing child to be home, 110, 114–117; deciding if child is ready, 110–112; making home safer, 117–120; neighborhood resources, 112–113; staying in touch by telephone, 113–114

American Association of University Women, 178

American Automobile Association, 90

American Home Economics Association, 150

Anger, parents', 15–16

Answering machines, to screen out telephone calls, 120

Art, 163

Attitude Survey, xiii-xiv

Baby sitters, 97, 98–103; checklist for, 103–104

Basic Aid Training, 178

Bedtime, 51–53

Bicycling to school, precautions about, 90

Big Red "E" Program, 176–177

Block Mother Program, 177

Boy Scouts of America, 180

Breakfast, 81, 82, 84; school system serving, 86

Briggs, Dorothy, *Your Child's Self-Esteem*, 22

Bus, school or public, 90–91

Callers, unexpected, 130–131

Care giver(s), 108–109; baby sitters as, 98–103; checklist for, 103–104; parents alternating as, 105; shared, 106. *See also* Child care

Child care: baby sitters, 98–104; group programs, 106–109; parents alternating as care givers, 105; programs supplying early morning, 86; relatives, 96–98; after school, 95–96. *See also* Care giver(s)

187